**MASTER FORMS & CONTRACTS
FROM YOUR COPIER**

Entrepreneurs,
Small Businesses

&

Landlords

*Robert Burns
&
Rees Johnson*

KNIGHT-RIDDER
PRESS

Tucson, Arizona

Published by Knight-Ridder Press
A Division of HPBooks, Inc.
P.O. Box 5367
Tucson, AZ 85703

Printed in U.S.A.
10 9 8 7 6 5 4 3 2
1st Printing

Library of Congress Cataloging in Publication Data

Burns, Robert, 1938-
    Master forms & contracts from your copier.

    1. Business—Forms.   2. Contracts—United
States—Forms. I. Johnson, Rees C., 1938- . II.
Title. III. Title: Master forms & contracts from
your copier.
HF5371.B845   1986   651'.29   86-82238
ISBN 0-89586-513-0

Acknowledgment

A very special thanks to Dee Burns, for putting up with a lot more than was necessary and for being the best of critics.

And a tip of our hats to Jerry Neilson, Gus Hill, and John Hasty at B. Laser Graphics, Portland, Oregon. They did a terrific job of designing the forms.

Other Knight-Ridder Press
Titles of Interest

Master Forms & Contracts From Your Copier:
Personal Finance & Home Management
Burns & Johnson (ISBN 0-89586-512-2)

INSURANCE: What Do You Need? How Much Is Enough?
Kennedy (ISBN 0-89586-436-3)

INCREASING YOUR WEALTH
A Professional Portfolio Manager Tells You How
Lerner & Koff (ISBN 0-89586-516-5)

Personal Economics
TAKE COMMAND OF YOUR MONEY AND
DEVELOP A WINNING FINANCIAL PLAN
Watts & Kennedy (ISBN 0-89586-517-3)

About The Authors

Robert Burns graduated from Portland State University with a degree in Business Administration and has over 20 years of experience in financial administration. He is presently Manager of the Multco Employee's Credit Union in Portland, Oregon and previously managed the Food and Agriculture Organization Credit Union in Rome, Italy. Specializing in family financial counseling, Mr. Burns has presented at numerous local, regional, and national conferences and is a frequent lecturer in the areas of financial counseling and management techniques at Mt. Hood Community College. He has blended his many experiences to help create this book.

Rees Johnson received his B.A. from Yale College in 1963, his J.D. from Yale Law School in 1966, and was admitted to practice law in the State of Oregon in 1967. Johnson is a senior partner in the firm of Shannon and Johnson. He has been extensively involved in small business and family estate planning and has written *Wills and Estate Planning,* currently in its second printing. As a recognized expert, Mr. Johnson is a frequent lecturer on family and small-business matters and is also actively involved in a number of consumer organizations and senior citizens' groups.

Contents

How To Use This Book

This is one of a series of books of master forms, contracts, and worksheets for use by the entrepreneur, owner of a small business, or landlord owning from one to ten rental units. Essentially, this book is a problem solver for just about everyone.

It is a unique combination of legal and personal stationery store, quick-print shop, and law office. It puts numerous documents, forms, and worksheets at your fingertips along with detailed information on where, when, and how to use them. All you need is this book, a photocopy machine, and a few nickels and dimes to buy the copies you need.

The forms in this book are for simple, straightforward transactions. For complex transactions or where substantial sums of money are involved, you should consult an attorney. To help you complete an unfamiliar form, all "legalese" is translated into plain English. And there are lots of clearly explained examples.

Nobody will use all of the forms and charts, but when you want a credit application, a bill of sale, or a purchase order to buy something at wholesale, it is difficult to find a substitute for the right one. The book has five different sections that will make your life a bit easier:

Management Aids

Big corporations can afford their own print shops and special forms, contracts, and worksheets. With this book, you can now be on an equal footing. This first section contains 14 forms designed to make many day-by-day chores easier and more profitable. For example, you can photocopy three different forms to help make using the telephone more efficient, or use another form to keep vital income tax records.

Dealing with Customers and Employees

Being in business means dealing with customers and employees. This section contains a number of forms to help with these two very important aspects of entrepreneuring. Making life easier and keeping you on the right legal path are the objectives of three employment applications and two credit applications found in this section. Also included are past-due notices ranging from gentle reminders to final notices, and several useful payroll forms.

Doing Business

Business runs on paper and documentation. The government, your customers, your vendors, and almost everyone else passes paperwork to your business. In turn, you must pass just as much paperwork on to your customers. Professional-looking statements, invoices, receipts, and estimates can mean the difference between being ignored by an important client and being noticed.

The purchase order is just one of the nearly 30 forms in this section that can save you time and money. By personalizing a purchase order, you can easily gain entry into hundreds of thousands of wholesale operations in this country. Joe Jones, Entrepreneur, can probably buy house paint at a realistic wholesale price much easier than Joe Jones, average citizen and householder.

Legal Issues

You can easily save substantial sums of money by using a legal form from this section. All are in plain, understandable language. They consist of an affidavit, an agreement, receipt formats, bills of sale, three powers of attorney, six versions of promissory notes, plus a number of other valuable and useful legal documents.

For example, suppose you are part of a couple who jointly owns property that is for sale or lease. If one of you is often away from home, you can use a form giving special limited power of attorney. With it, one spouse can delegate to the other all the powers necessary to complete a specific real estate transaction.

This section tells about signature requirements, notary publics, and the like. A number of forms are shown as if fully completed. Wherever necessary, a completion key gives you a line-by-line explanation. Be sure to read this section very carefully.

Landlording

Many people own rental property. Most own just one or two units and probably lose money each year due to poor recordkeeping. If you manage a few properties, this book will save you from such grief. It puts 22 valuable forms and worksheets at your fingertips. Starting with the all-important Rental Application, this book includes statements, notices, and bookkeeping worksheets—almost every piece of paper you need to be a successful owner/manager of income property.

Personalizing Your Forms

With a product from the 3M Corporation, you can easily personalize many of your forms. Most office-supply houses stock Post-it Cover-up Tape®, a close cousin of their famous yellow Post-it Notes®. This product is a white-opaque tape that comes in rolls in four different widths. Its main purpose is to block out unwanted material, like the page numbers on the forms in this book. Or, you can add typed corrections to originals.

Let's say you want a book of personalized receipts. Take a piece of the widest (1 inch) tape. Put it on an ordinary sheet of paper and type in your name, address, or other information. Apply the personalized tape to the master form. Because the cover-up tape can easily peel off, it's simple to change a form.

Or you can use a business card to personalize the forms in Sections II, III and V. Attach the card to the space provided and you'll make documents that give instant credibility.

Using a Copier

Since there are several hundred different copiers in use, we won't try to give you specific lessons. However, here are a few tips that can improve the quality of any copy.

● Make sure the glass is clean. Have you ever seen black spots on all of your copies in the same place? They could be spots floating in front of your eyes, but probably not. More than likely they are fingerprints, dirt, or flakes of correction fluid on the copier glass. A clean glass will almost always insure better, cleaner, crisper photocopies.

● If your copy has a dark area around one or more of the edges, it probably means that the original is slightly smaller than the field of vision of the copier. Prevent this by placing a larger piece of clean white paper on top of the original. Snugly close the lid of the copier over both.

● If you are going to copy without removing the perforated form from the book, be sure to press the entire master form as flat as possible. This might slightly bend the spine of the book but should prevent the inside edge of your copy from looking like it is "floating."

● Before tearing out a page at the perforations, bend it back and forth several times at the seam. This makes removal much easier and neater.

● File used originals in a large envelope with cardboard stiffening. Used and stored with a little care, these master forms should last for years.

Please Note

You are welcome to make as many copies as you wish of any form in this book. You are encouraged to give them away, to lend this book to others, or to use the forms in your business. However, you are not authorized to copy and then resell any form from this book. That is against the law.

We are eager to hear from you. We would appreciate any comments on improving these forms or adding particularly useful ones in a revision. Please send your comments to us in care of the Publisher.

SECTION I
Management Aids

Few people work harder than the owner(s) of a small business. Those of us who work for others can hardly understand the hours of sweat, worry and lost sleep that goes with being the boss or self-employed. Yet, in spite of all their efforts, 80% of all small businesses fail. In addition, most landlords don't take all of their legitimate tax deductions.

It is hard to wear the hats of bookkeeper, mechanic, janitor, sales rep, warehouser and others at the same time. Therefore, good management aids can help tie some loose ends together. And that's what the forms in this section are for. They are essential problem-solvers that will make your work a little easier.

"Neither a borrower nor a lender be" is considered sage advice, but it's not always practical. Even between family members or friends, everyone would probably feel more comfortable when a transaction is properly documented. (Several formats for promissory notes can be found in the legal forms section of this book.)

Give one copy of this Payment Book and keep the other yourself. It encourages good recordkeeping and helps settle misunderstandings.

Assuming that you will use the common monthly-interest method, you can calculate each month's interest with the following simple steps.

1) Take the interest rate and move the decimal point by two places to the left. For example, an interest rate of 14.5% becomes .145.

2) Divide the stated interest rate by 12, giving the interest rate for each month. For example, .145/12 = .0120833.

3) If you round the number to six places (.012083) you'll be accurate to the penny on large loans. If you round the number to five places (.01208) you'll be accurate enough for loans less than $1000. Write the rounded off number down in your payment book. You won't have to calculate it again unless the interest rate changes.

4) Multiply this number (.012083) by the last month's ending balance and you get the monthly interest due for that month. For example, if you still owe $12,450 on the loan, the monthly interest due (in addition to the monthly payment on the principal) is $12,450 x .012083 = $150.43.

Hint

Don't worry about computing interest on cents of the principal balance. If you round both upward and downward to the nearest whole dollar, it is unlikely that the difference in total interest paid would amount to more than a couple of pennies over the life of a typical loan.

PAYMENT BOOK

Payment Record for 19 _____

Borrower _____

Month Due	Date Paid	Amount Paid	Credited		Balance of Unpaid Principal
			Interest	Principal	
JAN					
FEB					
MAR					
APR					
MAY					
JUN					
JUL					
AUG					
SEP					
OCT					
NOV					
DEC					

PAYMENT BOOK

Payment Record for 19 _____

Borrower _____

Month Due	Date Paid	Amount Paid	Credited		Balance of Unpaid Principal
			Interest	Principal	
JAN					
FEB					
MAR					
APR					
MAY					
JUN					
JUL					
AUG					
SEP					
OCT					
NOV					
DEC					

PAYMENT BOOK

Payment Record for 19 _____

Borrower _____

Month Due	Date Paid	Amount Paid	Credited		Balance of Unpaid Principal
			Interest	Principal	
JAN					
FEB					
MAR					
APR					
MAY					
JUN					
JUL					
AUG					
SEP					
OCT					
NOV					
DEC					

PAYMENT BOOK

Payment Record for 19 _____

Borrower _____

Month Due	Date Paid	Amount Paid	Credited		Balance of Unpaid Principal
			Interest	Principal	
JAN					
FEB					
MAR					
APR					
MAY					
JUN					
JUL					
AUG					
SEP					
OCT					
NOV					
DEC					

If you have lent money, chances are that the borrower would need proof of the amount of interest paid. This form provides the evidence required by the Internal Revenue Service and also recaps all of the transactions for the year.

Hint

Make sure you keep a copy of the form for your own records. It could be valuable in the event of a later dispute.

STATEMENT OF INTEREST PAID

This is to certify that between January 1, 19 _____ and December 31, 19 _____

_____ paid $ _____ in interest on a

loan dated _____, 19 _____.

_____
(SIGNATURE OF LENDER)

_____
(PRINT LENDER'S NAME)

_____
(LENDER'S ADDRESS)

RECAP FOR 19 _____

BEGINNING PRINCIPAL BALANCE $ _____

DATE RECEIVED	TOTAL PAID	INTEREST	PRINCIPAL

ENDING PRINCIPAL BALANCE $ _____

STATEMENT OF INTEREST PAID

This is to certify that between January 1, 19 _____ and December 31, 19 _____

_____ paid $ _____ in interest on a

loan dated _____, 19 _____.

_____
(SIGNATURE OF LENDER)

_____
(PRINT LENDER'S NAME)

_____
(LENDER'S ADDRESS)

RECAP FOR 19 _____

BEGINNING PRINCIPAL BALANCE $ _____

DATE RECEIVED	TOTAL PAID	INTEREST	PRINCIPAL

ENDING PRINCIPAL BALANCE $ _____

Airlines handle tens of thousands of "frequent flier" transactions each day. It is not surprising that hundreds of these mileage credits slip between the cracks. You can easily keep your own verification records by using this mileage register.

Hint

Use one form for each airline and staple it to an envelope. When you have completed a journey, tuck the final carbon copy of the ticket into the envelope. You now have double proof of the trip, a log of your travels, and the copy of the actual tickets. In case of a dispute, it will probably be all you need to get it quickly and fairly settled.

Hint

Use airport designations in the "To/From" column. Airlines readily understand LAX/SEA to mean Los Angeles International Airport to Seattle-Tacoma International Airport.

AIRLINE MILEAGE REGISTER

_____ Airline

DATE	TO / FROM	TICKET #	MILES
	/		
	/		
	/		
	/		
	/		
	/		
	/		
	/		
	/		
	/		
	/		
	/		
	/		
	/		
	/		
	/		
	/		
	/		
	/		
	/		
	/		
	/		
TOTAL →			

AIRLINE MILEAGE REGISTER

_____ Airline

DATE	TO / FROM	TICKET #	MILES
	/		
	/		
	/		
	/		
	/		
	/		
	/		
	/		
	/		
	/		
	/		
	/		
	/		
	/		
	/		
	/		
	/		
	/		
	/		
	/		
	/		
	/		
TOTAL →			

BUSINESS EXPENSE RECORD

If you are self-employed, operate a part-time business, or are employed and spend your own money for travel, transportation, or entertainment expenses, you need accurate expense records. You may also need to verify expenses so you can submit timely and accurate claims for reimbursement.

The best source of information concerning complicated tax matters is either a tax expert or accurate publications. There are a number of official pamphlets that can be requested from the IRS. You call their toll-free number, usually found in the Yellow Pages under US Government-Internal Revenue Service.

The Internal Revenue Service can punish you for sloppy bookkeeping. If you attempt deductions that are later rejected, you may be subject to the tax, interest, and potential penalty. If you have complex problems involving these things, check with a lawyer or qualified tax specialist.

You may take a tax deduction for travel expenses if you are away from home for your business, profession, or job. Deductions for this purpose must be "reasonable," a requirement that may have to be defined later in the event of an audit.

As of this writing, deductible travel expenses include:

- Air, rail, and bus fares.
- Operating and maintaining your car.
- Taxi and other ground transportation costs if directly related to the purpose of your travel.
- Costs of transporting sample and display material.
- Meals and lodging while you are away from home on business.
- Cleaning and laundry.
- Business-related telephone and communication expenses.
- Incidental tips for any of the above expenses.

You can save some recordkeeping efforts by using the IRS standard daily meal allowance (the figure may change from year to year) for travel while away from home. To take a deduction for travel, you must be able to document:

1) All transportation, lodging, meal, and incidental expenses.
2) The dates you left and returned home.
3) Where you went.
4) The actual or expected business benefit gained from the trip.

If you use your own car for business purposes, you may deduct certain transportation costs. IRS rules and regulations concerning this type of expense are listed in its Publication 463. Most of the rules have to do with the business purpose (commuting costs are not deductible), split business and personal use, depreciation, and investment tax credits.

If your travel qualifies, you can deduct all or part of the costs of gas, oil, repairs, insurance, depreciation, interest to buy, taxes, licenses, and other incidental auto-related expenses. Instead of figuring actual expenses, consider using the IRS standard mileage rate, a figure that is published by the IRS and may change from year to year.

Documenting business entertainment expenses is a bit trickier and demands even more careful recordkeeping. The concept of "reasonableness" is the keystone. (Sorry, holding your Tupperware party in Paris after an evening on the town might not qualify.) You will need to prove:

1) The amount of each expense, except those incidental items (taxi, tips, telephone calls, etc.) that can be totaled on a daily basis.

2) The date of the entertainment.

3) Where and the type of entertainment deducted.

4) The actual or expected business benefit gained from the entertainment.

5) Enough information about the person being entertained to establish a sufficient business relationship.

There are several levels of proof that the IRS may require. Some simple expenses such as telephone calls, taxi fares, etc., can be summarized on a daily basis. You must document any expense over $25.00. Canceled checks and credit card receipts backed up by a business expense report are the most acceptable.

The actual regulations covering travel and entertainment expenses are too complex for discussion here. For more detailed information, refer to the IRS Publication that discusses travel, entertainment, and gift expenses.

BUSINESS EXPENSE RECORD

Name _____ For Week of _____ , to _____ , 19 _____

DESCRIPTION	SUN	MON	TUE	WED	THU	FRI	SAT	TOTAL
FOOD								
Breakfast								
Lunch								
Dinner								
Entertainment*								
_____								
LODGING								
Hotel								
Tel & tel								
_____								
TRANSPORTATION								
Air transportation**								
Auto rent								
Cab & tips								
Mile allowance***								
Gas & oil								
_____								
MISCELLANEOUS								
_____								
TOTAL EXPENSES								

* ENTERTAINMENT LOG

DATE	PLACE	PERSON(S)	COMPANY	AMOUNT
REMARKS				
REMARKS				
REMARKS				
REMARKS				

** AIR FARE EXPENSES

DATE	FLT #	FROM	VIA	TO	COST

*** MILEAGE ALLOWANCE - _____ . _____ cents per mile

	SUN	MON	TUE	WED	THU	FRI	SAT	TOTAL
End Mileage								
Start								
Driven today								

LOCAL AUTO MILEAGE EXPENSE

The IRS has one very firm rule: If you can't document it, you'd better not deduct it. When you manage a small business, it is very easy to lose track of the many trips you take by car. Short trips add up, and hundreds of dollars in legal and proper deductions can be lost due to poor paperwork. This form and a clipboard in your car can help recover some of these lost dollars.

LOCAL AUTO MILEAGE EXPENSE

EMPLOYEE NAME _____

FOR PERIOD _____ TO _____

_____ MILES AT $ _____ . ___ PER MILE $ _____ . ___

OTHER AUTO RELATED EXPENSES $ _____ . ___

LESS CASH ADVANCE ($ _____ . ___)

TOTAL REIMBURSEMENT $ _____ . ___

DATE	TRAVEL FROM	TRAVEL TO	ODOMETER		ACTUAL MILEAGE
			START	END	
				TOTAL MILES	

Even though they have been recently altered by Congress, Individual Retirement Accounts (IRAs), Keoghs, and deferred compensation plans still are probably the best deal around for most working people. Each plan has its own rules and regulations. The Internal Revenue Service can levy very stiff penalties if you put in more than allowed into your accounts. You can use this Annual Contribution Log to keep track of up to four accounts per page.

Hint

Be extra careful when transferring accounts from one institution to another. Particularly with IRAs—if they are not handled properly, the IRS could consider that you have received "constructive receipt" of the funds, making you subject to full taxation plus a 10% direct penalty.

ANNUAL PENSION CONTRIBUTION LOG

For Year of	Investment	☐ IRA ☐ Keogh ☐ Other

Month	Contribution	Earnings	Withdrawals
JAN			
FEB			
MAR			
APR			
MAY			
JUN			
JUL			
AUG			
SEP			
OCT			
NOV			
DEC			
Jan retro			
Feb retro			
Mar retro			
Apr retro			
TOTAL			

For Year of	Investment	☐ IRA ☐ Keogh ☐ Other

Month	Contribution	Earnings	Withdrawals
JAN			
FEB			
MAR			
APR			
MAY			
JUN			
JUL			
AUG			
SEP			
OCT			
NOV			
DEC			
Jan retro			
Feb retro			
Mar retro			
Apr retro			
TOTAL			

For Year of	Investment	☐ IRA ☐ Keogh ☐ Other

Month	Contribution	Earnings	Withdrawals
JAN			
FEB			
MAR			
APR			
MAY			
JUN			
JUL			
AUG			
SEP			
OCT			
NOV			
DEC			
Jan retro			
Feb retro			
Mar retro			
Apr retro			
TOTAL			

For Year of	Investment	☐ IRA ☐ Keogh ☐ Other

Month	Contribution	Earnings	Withdrawals
JAN			
FEB			
MAR			
APR			
MAY			
JUN			
JUL			
AUG			
SEP			
OCT			
NOV			
DEC			
Jan retro			
Feb retro			
Mar retro			
Apr retro			
TOTAL			

RECAP

Institution Investment	Beginning Balance	Contributions	Earnings	Withdrawals	Ending Balance
TOTAL FOR YEAR					

PHONE MESSAGE FORM

Businesses are not alone in benefiting from handy "While you were out" message forms. Photocopy several sheets, cut them apart, and leave several at each phone in the house.

TO		
DATE		TIME

WHILE YOU WERE OUT

M	
OF	
TELEPHONE NUMBER	

TELEPHONED		PLEASE CALL	
CALLED TO SEE YOU		WILL CALL AGAIN	
WANTS TO SEE YOU		RETURNED YOUR CALL	

MESSAGE

TO		
DATE		TIME

WHILE YOU WERE OUT

M	
OF	
TELEPHONE NUMBER	

TELEPHONED		PLEASE CALL	
CALLED TO SEE YOU		WILL CALL AGAIN	
WANTS TO SEE YOU		RETURNED YOUR CALL	

MESSAGE

TO		
DATE		TIME

WHILE YOU WERE OUT

M	
OF	
TELEPHONE NUMBER	

TELEPHONED		PLEASE CALL	
CALLED TO SEE YOU		WILL CALL AGAIN	
WANTS TO SEE YOU		RETURNED YOUR CALL	

MESSAGE

TO		
DATE		TIME

WHILE YOU WERE OUT

M	
OF	
TELEPHONE NUMBER	

TELEPHONED		PLEASE CALL	
CALLED TO SEE YOU		WILL CALL AGAIN	
WANTS TO SEE YOU		RETURNED YOUR CALL	

MESSAGE

PHONE CONTACT LOG

When doing battle with a large corporation, mail-order firm, or even a government office, have you ever had one person tell you what to do, and then another just the opposite? We have all experienced it.

When dealing with bureaucrats and clerks over the phone, put everything you can in writing—and let them know that you are doing so. Always get the individual's name, title, department, phone number, extension, and the exact time and date of the call. While this is not absolute proof, you will be pleasantly surprised at the weight that a phone diary carries with supervisors and even in a court of law.

Hint

Use the reverse of this form for a full and complete narrative of your conversation. A careful synopsis of your discussion can be a real aid in jogging memories.

PHONE CONTACT LOG

The Issue _____

_____ This is call # _____

I called _____ on _____
    (firm or government office)   (date)

at _____ AM/PM, at (___) ___ — _____ and talked to
(time)   (phone number)

_____ of the _____ dept.
(person)

Statements made by this person _____

Promises and committments made by this person _____

(I was referred) (My call was transferred) to _____

_____ of _____

My Comments _____

_____

This call took about _____ minutes and cost

(about) (exactly) $ _____ in toll charges.

Toll free number for future use: (800) _____ — _____

_____
(Signature of Caller)

PHONE CONTACT LOG

The Issue _____

_____ This is call # _____

I called _____ on _____
    (firm or government office)   (date)

at _____ AM/PM, at (___) ___ — _____ and talked to
(time)   (phone number)

_____ of the _____ dept.
(person)

Statements made by this person _____

Promises and committments made by this person _____

(I was referred) (My call was transferred) to _____

_____ of _____

My Comments _____

_____

This call took about _____ minutes and cost

(about) (exactly) $ _____ in toll charges.

Toll free number for future use: (800) _____ — _____

_____
(Signature of Caller)

DAILY TELEPHONE LOG

If yours is like most small businesses, you will spend a good part of your day with a telephone stuck to your ear. Some entrepreneurs do 100% of their business without ever seeing a real live customer or client!

It takes only a moment to keep a telephone log, but it can pay big dividends in sales, customer relations, and even differences that don't become disputes.

DAILY TELEPHONE LOG

DATE _____   BY _____

TO	FROM	PERSON	TEL #	COMMENTS	TIME
T	F				
T	F				
T	F				
T	F				
T	F				
T	F				
T	F				
T	F				
T	F				
T	F				
T	F				
T	F				
T	F				
T	F				
T	F				
T	F				
T	F				
T	F				
T	F				
T	F				
T	F				
T	F				
T	F				
T	F				

LONG DISTANCE PHONE CALL LOG

An unsupervised telephone is a potential sinkhole of wasted cash. Unauthorized callers, gabby employees, and telephone company mistakes can waste money.

But the biggest reason to keep good, long distance records is telephone fraud. Millions of dollars each year are incorrectly billed and paid (!) by unaware consumers.

LONG DISTANCE PHONE CALL LOG

DATE TIME	PHONE #	FIRM	PERSON	COMMENTS

People who plan ahead are usually the ones who get ahead. Planning is not easy unless you have a little help or are one of those very organized and disciplined persons.

We have included formats for a daily planner and a weekly planner. Do not be afraid to use both. Keep longer-term goals in view on the weekly format and use the daily planner as a guide through the limited working hours of each day.

Daily Planner and Record

For _____ The _____ Day Of _____ , 19 _____

7:00			**Baggage From Yesterday**
7:30			
8:00			
8:30			
9:00			
9:30			**Do Today**
10:00			1 _____
			2 _____
10:30			3 _____
			4 _____
11:00			5 _____
			6 _____
11:30			7 _____
			8 _____
12:00			9 _____
			10 _____
12:30			
1:00			
1:30			
2:00			**Look Ahead 30 Days**
2:30			
3:00			
3:30			
4:00			**Look Ahead 6 Months**
4:30			
5:00			
5:30			
6:00			**Personal - Family Events Planner**
6:30			
7:00			
8:00			
9:00			
10:00			
11:00			
12:00			

WEEKLY PLANNER AND RECORD

From _____ , to _____ , 19 _____ .

Monday _____ _____

_____ _____
_____ _____
_____ _____
_____ _____
_____ _____
_____ _____

Tuesday _____ _____

_____ _____
_____ _____
_____ _____
_____ _____
_____ _____
_____ _____
_____ _____

Wednesday _____ _____

_____ _____
_____ _____
_____ _____
_____ _____
_____ _____
_____ _____

Thursday _____ _____

_____ _____
_____ _____
_____ _____
_____ _____
_____ _____

Friday _____ _____

_____ _____
_____ _____
_____ _____
_____ _____
_____ _____
_____ _____

Saturday _____ _____

_____ _____
_____ _____
_____ _____

Sunday _____ _____

_____ _____
_____ _____
_____ _____

Baggage from Last Week

_____
_____
_____
_____
_____
_____

Do This Week

1 _____
2 _____
3 _____
4 _____
5 _____
6 _____
7 _____
8 _____
9 _____
10 _____

_____
_____

LOOK AHEAD 30 Days

_____
_____
_____
_____

LOOK AHEAD 6 Months

_____
_____
_____
_____
_____

Personal-Family Events Planner

_____
_____
_____
_____
_____

SECTION II
Forms for Customers and Employees

A lot of people start a business to be their own boss, but it seems that the owner of a small business is the most "bossed" person in business. Clients, customers, employees, competitors, bankers, unions, inspectors, officials and more seem to want a small piece of the entrepreneur.

Though no form or worksheet will solve your people matters, they can help you professionally maintain these most important relationships.

EMPLOYMENT APPLICATIONS

As the owner of a small business, you must wear many hats. The hat of the personnel manager is perhaps the most difficult because a hiring mistake can be costly. You can spend a lot of time and money advertising, recruiting, interviewing, checking, and finally adding an employee to your payroll. If an employee lasts for only a few days or weeks, it is money down the drain.

Laws

During the hiring process, be sure to obey the law. Particularly at the federal level, there are a number of laws and regulations directly affecting the hiring process. These regulations include:

- Title VII of the Civil Rights Act of 1964, which deals with discrimination due to race, color, religion, sex, or national origin.
- The Equal Pay Act of 1963, which treats the issue of equal pay for men and women doing the same work.
- The Age Discrimination in Employment Act of 1967, which requires that you do not discriminate in your hiring practices against workers between 40 and 70.

You can be reasonably safe by using some common sense and being fair. Don't set job standards artificially high, particularly if people with lesser experience are already doing the same job. This is also true for setting education standards. They must be reasonable for the task. If you require two years of college for a relatively unskilled job, it could be charged that your standards are deliberately set to exclude minorities, women, and many older workers.

Three Forms

We have provided three specialized employment applications. The first is specifically designed for high-school and college students. When hiring young people, you usually have little in the way of employment history to verify. This application asks some questions that could help you make a good hiring decision.

The second application is more complex and uses most of the standard questions found on corporate employment applications. Use it when you want to make a thorough background verification. The last application is one page long and asks only essential questions. It could be useful as a prescreening device and when you are hiring short-term or temporary employees.

Hint

Keep employment applications for several years. You may have to defend yourself, and having accurate records of the persons who have applied could be useful.

APPLICATION FOR EMPLOYMENT
(STUDENT)

We fully comply with all federal and state laws concerning employment without regard to race, religion, color, or national origin.

Name _____ Social Security _____ Phone (____) _____

Address _____ City _____ State _____ Zip _____

How long at this address? _____ Previous address _____

What would you like to do for us? _____ When can you start? _____

Available:
- [ ] Monday
- [ ] Tuesday
- [ ] Wednesday
- [ ] Thursday
- [ ] Friday
- [ ] Saturday
- [ ] Sunday
- [ ] Days
- [ ] Evenings
- [ ] Nights
- [ ] Holidays
- [ ] _____

School Information

Name and location	Yr attending	Grad?	GPA	Major
High School _____	9 - 10 - 11 - 12	Y N		
Community College _____	13 - 14	Y N		
College _____	13 - 14 - 15 - 16	Y N		

Vocational/Special Interests

Mark   1=very interested.   2=somewhat interested.   3=no interest at all.

- [ ] Agriculture
- [ ] Art
- [ ] Athletics
- [ ] Computer Science
- [ ] Drama
- [ ] English
- [ ] History
- [ ] Horticulture
- [ ] Foreign Language
- [ ] Math
- [ ] Music
- [ ] Office skills
- [ ] Science
- [ ] Shop
- [ ] Social studies
- [ ] _____

Comments _____

List two school references - counselors, teachers, etc.

_____

_____

Work Experience - List name, position, person to contact.

1. _____

2. _____

_____

Valid Driver's License? ☐ Y ☐ N What state? _____ Valid auto insurance? ☐ Y ☐ N

Physical handicaps preventing you from doing certain work? ☐ Y ☐ N   (If yes, explain on reverse)

Message Phone: Days (_____) _____ Evenings (_____) _____

Date _____   X _____

Use reverse for additional details.

APPLICATION FOR EMPLOYMENT

We fully comply with all federal and state laws concerning employment without regard to race, religion, color, or national origin.

Name _____ Social Security _____ Phone (___) _____

Address _____ City _____ State _____ Zip _____

How long at this address? _____ Previous address _____

What would you like to do for us? _____ When can you start? _____

School Information

Name and location	Last year attended?	Grad?	GPA	Major
High School _____	9-10-11-12	Y N		
Community College _____	13-14	Y N		
College _____	13-14-15-16	Y N		
Technical/Trade _____		Y N		

Employment History - Present employer first.

Company name Phone number	Address Supervisor	Dates From-to	Why Did You Leave?
		Job Description	

Company name Phone number	Address Supervisor	Dates From-to	Why Did You Leave?
		Job Description	

Company name Phone number	Address Supervisor	Dates From-to	Why Did You Leave?
		Job Description	

Valid Driver's License? ☐ Y ☐ N What state? _____ Valid auto insurance? ☐ Y ☐ N

Physical handicaps preventing you from doing certain work? ☐ Y ☐ N (If yes, explain on reverse)

Message Phone: Days (_____) _____ Evenings (_____) _____

Date _____ X _____

Use reverse for additional details.

Have you ever been refused bond? ☐ Yes* ☐ No

Have you ever had a bond revoked? ☐ Yes* ☐ No

Have you ever been convicted of a crime in the past 10 years? ☐ Yes* ☐ No

Do you have any physical handicaps preventing you from doing certain types of work? ☐ Yes* ☐ No

Have you had any serious illnesses in the past five years? ☐ Yes* ☐ No

Do you hold a valid driver's license?
(If yes, classification and/or restrictions)
_____ ☐ Yes ☐ No

Do you have auto liability insurance in force? ☐ Yes ☐ No

* Explain

MILITARY SERVICE

Branch _____ Rank _____ Type of discharge _____

Date entered _____ Date discharged _____

Special training, education, duties, awards, commendations. _____

_____

_____

_____

BUSINESS REFERENCES

Name _____ Address _____

City, State, ZIP _____ Phone _____

Name _____ Address _____

City, State, ZIP _____ Phone _____

Name _____ Address _____

City, State, ZIP _____ Phone _____

PERSONAL REFERENCES

Name _____ Address _____

City, State, ZIP _____ Phone _____

Name _____ Address _____

City, State, ZIP _____ Phone _____

Name _____ Address _____

City, State, ZIP _____ Phone _____

The information provided by me in this application is true and complete to the best of my knowledge. I understand that if I am employed, any false statements will be considered as cause for possible dismissal. You are hereby authorized to conduct any investigation of my personal history and/or credit and financial records employing investigative or credit agencies or bureaus of your choice subject to the provisions of the Fair Credit Reporting Act.

Message Phone: Days (_____) _____ Evenings (_____) _____

Date _____ X _____

APPLICATION FOR EMPLOYMENT

We fully comply with all federal and state laws concerning employment without regard to race, religion, color, or national origin.

Name _____ Social Security _____ Phone (____) _____

Address _____ City _____ State ____ Zip _____

How long at this address? _____ Previous address _____

What would you like to do for us? _____ When can you start? _____

School Information

Name and location	Last year attended?	Grad?	GPA	Major
High School _____	9 - 10 - 11 - 12	Y N		
Community College _____	13 - 14	Y N		
College _____	13 - 14 - 15 - 16	Y N		
Technical/Trade _____		Y N		

Employment History - Present employer first.

Company name Phone number	Address Supervisor	Dates From-to	Why Did You Leave?
		Job Description	

Company name Phone number	Address Supervisor	Dates From-to	Why Did You Leave?
		Job Description	

Company name Phone number	Address Supervisor	Dates From-to	Why Did You Leave?
		Job Description	

Company name Phone number	Address Supervisor	Dates From-to	Why Did You Leave?
		Job Description	

WEEKLY TIME CARD

A time card is a vital document in most payroll systems. It lists the regular hours and overtime hours worked by your employees. It is very important that each time card be signed by the employee.

Some other reasons for keeping time cards include:

1) It is the basic accounting document needed to compute an employee's gross wages due.

2) In some states, certain unemployment compensation taxes are computed on the total hours worked, a figure readily available on this weekly time card.

3) As the form is signed by the employee, it provides a substantial proof of expenditure in the event of an audit by the Internal Revenue Service.

4) If you hire younger employees, most states have restrictive regulations concerning the number of hours they are permitted to work, the time of day or night, and the type of work. A signed time card can prove compliance with many of these regulations.

ABOUT PAYROLL RECORDS

The IRS, Department of Labor and many state and local authorities require that you retain payroll records. Although each jurisdiction determines the number of years you are required to keep records, most require four-year retention.

It is prudent to keep them an extra year just in case. Any records dealing with pensions must be maintained indefinitely. For precise identification, always be sure that all documents relating to a particular employee contain his or her Social Security number.

WEEKLY TIME CARD

I CERTIFY THESE HOURS TO BE CORRECT

EMPLOYEE _____ X

SOCIAL SECURITY NUMBER _____ _____ DATE _____

PAY PERIOD: SUNDAY_____,19_____ TO SATURDAY_____,19_____.

	REGULAR TIME		REGULAR TIME		OVERTIME		TOTAL HOURS WORKED	
	IN	OUT	IN	OUT	IN	OUT	REGULAR	OVERTIME
SUN								
MON								
TUE								
WED								
THU								
FRI								
SAT								

WEEKLY TIME CARD

I CERTIFY THESE HOURS TO BE CORRECT

EMPLOYEE _____ X

SOCIAL SECURITY NUMBER _____ _____ DATE _____

PAY PERIOD: SUNDAY_____,19_____ TO SATURDAY_____,19_____.

	REGULAR TIME		REGULAR TIME		OVERTIME		TOTAL HOURS WORKED	
	IN	OUT	IN	OUT	IN	OUT	REGULAR	OVERTIME
SUN								
MON								
TUE								
WED								
THU								
FRI								
SAT								

WEEKLY TIME CARD

I CERTIFY THESE HOURS TO BE CORRECT

EMPLOYEE _____ X

SOCIAL SECURITY NUMBER _____ _____ DATE _____

PAY PERIOD: SUNDAY_____,19_____ TO SATURDAY_____,19_____.

	REGULAR TIME		REGULAR TIME		OVERTIME		TOTAL HOURS WORKED	
	IN	OUT	IN	OUT	IN	OUT	REGULAR	OVERTIME
SUN								
MON								
TUE								
WED								
THU								
FRI								
SAT								

PAYROLL STATEMENT

This payroll statement serves double duty. First, it is a weekly, bi-weekly, or monthly statement given to the employee with his or her check. Second, it can serve as a payroll summary. At the end of each quarter, you can add all the weekly statements and note the figures on a statement. These figures give the information you need to complete the necessary forms to remit to IRS, Social Security Administration, and to your state income tax and employment tax agencies.

Each figure of the Payroll Statement is important. Use great care when completing the form. Accurately maintained payroll records are of key importance when trying to resolve future inquiries from the employee, IRS, Social Security Administration, or any involved state and local taxing authorities. Always complete this form in carbon duplicate.

Hint

If your handwriting is not always clear, enter dates in the *July 6, 1988* format rather than *7-6-88*. The most important number on the form is the employee's Social Security identification number. It ties all of your and your employees' records together. Take care to make it always correct.

PAYROLL STATEMENT

EMPLOYEE_____   OT HOURS _____   OT RATE $ _____
S. S. # _____|_____|_____ DEPENDENTS _____   NET AMOUNT PAID TO EMPLOYEE $ _____
REG HOURS_____ REG RATE $ _____   PREPAID BY _____   DATE _____

EARNINGS			DEDUCTIONS		PAY PERIOD
REGULAR WAGES			FEDERAL WH TAXES		FROM _____
OVERTIME WAGES			STATE WH TAXES		TO _____
TIPS			FED INS. CONTRIB		DATE _____
			STATE UNEMPLOY		PREPARED BY
			STATE DISABILITY		
					_____
TOTAL EARNINGS			TOTAL DEDUCTIONS		

PAYROLL STATEMENT

EMPLOYEE_____   OT HOURS _____   OT RATE $ _____
S. S. # _____|_____|_____ DEPENDENTS _____   NET AMOUNT PAID TO EMPLOYEE $ _____
REG HOURS_____ REG RATE $ _____   PREPAID BY _____   DATE _____

EARNINGS			DEDUCTIONS		PAY PERIOD
REGULAR WAGES			FEDERAL WH TAXES		FROM _____
OVERTIME WAGES			STATE WH TAXES		TO _____
TIPS			FED INS. CONTRIB		DATE _____
			STATE UNEMPLOY		PREPARED BY
			STATE DISABILITY		
					_____
TOTAL EARNINGS			TOTAL DEDUCTIONS		

PAYROLL STATEMENT

EMPLOYEE_____   OT HOURS _____   OT RATE $ _____
S. S. # _____|_____|_____ DEPENDENTS _____   NET AMOUNT PAID TO EMPLOYEE $ _____
REG HOURS_____ REG RATE $ _____   PREPAID BY _____   DATE _____

EARNINGS			DEDUCTIONS		PAY PERIOD
REGULAR WAGES			FEDERAL WH TAXES		FROM _____
OVERTIME WAGES			STATE WH TAXES		TO _____
TIPS			FED INS. CONTRIB		DATE _____
			STATE UNEMPLOY		PREPARED BY
			STATE DISABILITY		
					_____
TOTAL EARNINGS			TOTAL DEDUCTIONS		

EMPLOYEE ATTENDANCE

It takes only a few moments to transcribe information from an employee's weekly time card to an annual recap. Here are a few reasons to maintain this form:

1) Keep track of earned and used vacation time.
2) Spot trends in excessive sick leave or unexcused absences.
3) Use as documentation for discharge due to poor attendance.

Hint

This not-unusual story is a very common reason to keep an Employee Attendance Record. Nearly two years after an employee leaves, you receive a notice from your State Wage and Hour Commission that you owe thousands of dollars in overtime and unpaid vacation. Because you have long since discarded your records, there is no choice but to pay.

EMPLOYEE ATTENDANCE

EMPLOYEE _____ SOC. SEC. # _____

DEPARTMENT _____ EMPLOYEE # _____

	JAN	FEB	MAR	APR	MAY	JUN	JUL	AUG	SEP	OCT	NOV	DEC
1												
2												
3												
4												
5												
6												
7												
8												
9												
10												
11												
12												
13												
14												
15												
16												
17												
18												
19												
20												
21												
22												
23												
24												
25												
26												
27												
28												
29												
30		▓										
31		▓		▓		▓	▓		▓		▓	

ANNUAL RECAP													TOTAL
EA													
UA													
S													
FS													
V													
JD													
ML													
LA													

EA	=	EXCUSED ABSENCE		UA	=	UNEXCUSED ABSENCE
S	=	SICKNESS		FS	=	FAMILY SICKNESS
V	=	VACATION		JD	=	JURY DUTY
ML	=	MILITARY LEAVE		LA	=	LEAVE OF ABSENCE (W/O PAY)

CREDIT APPLICATIONS

The very fact that you are using a credit application will have some bearing on potential applicants. If an applicant complains or is reluctant to provide verifiable information, consider it a good indication that you might be better off withholding credit.

Two credit applications are provided here, one for individuals and one for companies. They are similar to those used by a department store or bank and ask all of the usual questions concerning name, address, job, income, and credit references.

Now that you have a completed credit application, what should you do with it? First, read it carefully and make sure it is complete. A reluctant applicant might avoid revealing an important bit of information. Next, use a little common sense. You may be able to qualify the applicant yourself with a few probing questions and a phone call or two. Don't bother checking personal references. Would you list someone who would say anything negative?

Finally, consider an investment in information. You can ask a local credit-reporting agency for a credit report. It can be one of the most worthwhile investments ever made, particularly if it weeds out those with a "no pay" history.

Look in the Yellow Pages under "Credit Bureaus" or "Credit Reporting Agencies." Unless you are a member or regular user, however, it is often not easy to secure a credit report. The applicant will have to authorize the reporting agency to release the information to you, and you will have to certify that any information is for the purpose of entering into a credit agreement and will not be divulged to outside parties. Each credit application provided has the appropriate wording and room for the signatures of both parties.

If your personal investigation reveals no positive information and if the credit bureau comes up with a "no file" or a very limited file, consider the applicant carefully. It may be in your long-term best interest to look for another credit customer with a verifiable track record.

ABOUT CREDIT FORMS

According to many small-business experts, the three most important ingredients for success are location, good bookkeeping, and tight credit policies. The only disagreement among the experts is the order of importance of these ingredients. No matter which theory you subscribe to, it is undeniable that if you must advance credit, you must do so wisely.

The requirement for most small-business persons is simple: They want a customer who can, and will, pay per the agreed terms. Although there is no magic wand that helps in the selection decision, there is some advice that has been around in the credit business for decades. Any applicant must be of good character and have the capacity to meet the terms of the credit agreement.

Let's analyze character and capacity. First, character is another word for the applicant's past history. If an applicant has never paid a bill in his life, owes every merchant in town, and has dozens of suits and collections on file, it is likely (but not 100% guaranteed) that he will not pay you any better than he has paid anyone else.

Likewise, if an applicant has a history of steady income and meeting his bills and obligations promptly, it is likely (but not 100% guaranteed) that these paying habits will continue.

Having the capacity to pay simply means that the applicant has a steady source of income sufficient to meet all business and family obligations. You can verify capacity by knowing something about the business or employment record and making a judgment on the potential of continued income.

There are several ways to verify both character and capacity. They may take a little time and money, but are well worth it when compared to the potential losses of a non-paying customer.

CREDIT APPLICATION
Personal

PLEASE PRINT --- ALL information must be completed. The decision to grant credit will depend in great part on your credit history and references. Use the back for additional information.

PERSONAL INFORMATION

Name _____ Date of Birth _____

Phone _____ Soc. Sec. # ___ ___ ___ ___ Driver's Lic. _____ State _____

Present Address _____ City _____ State ____ Zip _____

How long at this address? _____ years _____ months. Phone (_____) _____

Landlord/Mortgagor _____ Month $ _____

Prev Address _____ City _____ State _____ How Long? _____

Employer _____ Position _____ How Long? _____

Address _____ Phone _____

Former Employer _____ Position _____ How Long? _____

Address _____ Phone _____

CREDIT REFERENCES

Bank/CU _____ Acct #(s) _____ Branch _____

City _____ State _____ How long _____ Check ____ Save ____ Loan ____

Bank/CU _____ Acct #(s) _____ Branch _____

City _____ State _____ How long _____ Check ____ Save ____ Loan ____

Other active reference _____ Acct. # _____

City _____ State _____ How long _____ Type of Acct. _____

Other active reference _____ Acct. # _____

City _____ State _____ How long _____ Type of Acct. _____

Other active reference _____ Acct. # _____

City _____ State _____ How long _____ Type of Acct. _____

Other active reference _____ Acct. # _____

City _____ State _____ How long _____ Type of Acct. _____

I give my permission for any credit reporting agency to release my file to undersigned Creditor for the purposes of entering into a credit agreement. I further authorize the undersigned Creditor or his agents to verify the above information including but not limited to contacting applicant's credit references, both listed herein or not, and personal references.

Dated _____ , 19 _____   Applicant: _____

Creditor's Agreement

We acknowledge that this information is strictly for the purposes of making a credit decision and agree that any verifications are for this purpose only and further agree that any information derived from credit reports and other verifications will be kept confidential and not revealed to any outside party.

CREDIT APPLICATION
Company

PLEASE PRINT --- ALL information must be completed. The decision to grant credit will depend in great part on your credit history and references. Use the back for additional information.

PERSONAL INFORMATION - Business principals (For identification only)

Name _____ Date of Birth _____ Phone _____
Title/position _____ Soc. Sec. # _____
Present Address _____ City _____ State _____ Zip _____

Name _____ Date of Birth _____ Phone _____
Title/position _____ Soc. Sec. # _____
Present Address _____ City _____ State _____ Zip _____

BUSINESS INFORMATION

☐ Sole proprietorship ☐ Partnership ☐ D&B # _____
☐ Corporation - State of _____ . Year incorporated _____

CREDIT REFERENCES

Bank _____ Acct #(s) _____ Branch _____
City _____ State _____ How long _____ Check _____ Save _____ Loan _____

Bank _____ Acct #(s) _____ Branch _____
City _____ State _____ How long _____ Check _____ Save _____ Loan _____

Other active reference _____ Acct. # _____
City _____ State _____ How long _____ Type of Acct. _____

Other active reference _____ Acct. # _____
City _____ State _____ How long _____ Type of Acct. _____

Other active reference _____ Acct. # _____
City _____ State _____ How long _____ Type of Acct. _____

Other active reference _____ Acct. # _____
City _____ State _____ How long _____ Type of Acct. _____

I give my permission for any credit reporting agency to release my file to undersigned Creditor for the purposes of entering into a credit agreement. I further authorize the undersigned Creditor or his agents to verify the above information including but not limited to contacting applicant's credit references, both listed herein or not, and personal references.

Applicant: _____

Dated _____ , 19 _____ Position/title _____

Creditor's Agreement

We acknowledge that this information is strictly for the purposes of making a credit decision and agree that any verifications are for this purpose only and further agree that any information derived from credit reports and other verifications will be kept confidential and not revealed to any outside party.

CREDIT INQUIRY

Many firms are reluctant to give any credit history over the phone to strangers. Still others report only to established credit-reporting services. Where a credit decision does not have to be made quickly, you may be able to do your own credit checking by using this credit inquiry.

CREDIT INQUIRY

Creditor

_____

_____

_____

_____

We would appreciate your providing us with a brief summary of your credit experience with:

_____

_____

_____

_____

We certify that this inquiry is for the purpose of entering into a credit arrangement and we further agree that any information derived from your response will be kept confidential and not revealed to any outside party.

Thank you,

- -

(Please tear off and return. Thank you.

CREDIT REPORT

Creditor _____   Debtor _____

Doing business with _____ years?   Largest balance $ _____

Terms _____   Present balance $ _____

General ☐ Takes discounts.   ☐ Prompt to _____ days slow.
recent ☐ Prompt.   ☐ Makes partial payments.
history ☐ Slightly slow.   ☐ Very slow.

Comments _____

_____

_____
(Signature of credit grantor)

COLLECTION NOTICES

If you have taken a chance and extended credit, you must have a firm billing and collection policy. One of the strongest weapons in your collection arsenal is predictability. A past due account, even a few days late, should be treated as a serious matter.

Once you establish a pattern of immediate reaction to a late payment, a "slow-pay" customer may well put your account a little higher on the payment priority list. We suggest that a first notice be sent between three and five days after the due date and a second notice between seven and ten days. Where a customer has a past history of serious delinquency, the second notice might be dropped in favor of an even stronger third notice.

Do not, however, continually threaten serious legal action unless you intend to follow through.

Hint

Making copies creates a permanent record of your collection activity.

DATE_____

FOR FURTHER INFO CALL:

_____

CUSTOMER # _____

BALANCE DUE $ _____

DUE DATE _____

JUST A REMINDER

_____

_____

_____

We haven't noted receipt of your check for the above balance. If you have already mailed it, please disregard this notice.

THANK YOU

DATE_____

FOR FURTHER INFO CALL:

_____

CUSTOMER # _____

BALANCE DUE $ _____

DUE DATE _____

JUST A REMINDER

_____

_____

_____

We haven't noted receipt of your check for the above balance. If you have already mailed it, please disregard this notice.

THANK YOU

DATE _____

FOR FURTHER INFO CALL:

_____

CUSTOMER # _____

BALANCE DUE $ _____

DUE DATE _____

_____

_____

_____

SECOND NOTICE

Is there a problem? We hope not. This is the second notice and we would appreciate the settlement of this balance.

THANK YOU

DATE _____

FOR FURTHER INFO CALL:

_____

CUSTOMER # _____

BALANCE DUE $ _____

DUE DATE _____

_____

_____

_____

SECOND NOTICE

Is there a problem? We hope not. This is the second notice and we would appreciate the settlement of this balance.

THANK YOU

DATE_____

FOR FURTHER INFO CALL:

_____

CUSTOMER # _____

BALANCE DUE $ _____

DUE DATE _____

_____

_____

_____   **THIRD NOTICE**

Frankly we are worried. We have sent you a statement and two reminders. This is the third.
Your immediate attention is required.

THANK YOU

DATE_____

FOR FURTHER INFO CALL:

_____

CUSTOMER # _____

BALANCE DUE $ _____

DUE DATE _____

_____

_____

_____   **THIRD NOTICE**

Frankly we are worried. We have sent you a statement and two reminders. This is the third.
Your immediate attention is required.

THANK YOU

DATE_____

FOR FURTHER INFO CALL:

_____

CUSTOMER # _____

BALANCE DUE $ _____

DUE DATE _____

_____

_____

_____

FINAL NOTICE

Our business and yours depend upon everyone's maintaining a good credit standing. Unless this matter is settled immediately, we will consider turning this past due account over to the attorneys of our collection agency.

DATE_____

FOR FURTHER INFO CALL:

_____

CUSTOMER # _____

BALANCE DUE $ _____

DUE DATE _____

_____

_____

_____

FINAL NOTICE

Our business and yours depend upon everyone's maintaining a good credit standing. Unless this matter is settled immediately, we will consider turning this past due account over to the attorneys of our collection agency.

DAILY SALES LOG

If your business involves sales and customer contacts, a daily sales log is a must. It is a score-card of today's accomplishments and a road map to tomorrow's activities. The effectiveness of a daily sales log can be increased by keeping it "where the action is." If the phone is your primary sales tool, keep the log close by. If you are on the outside most of the time, the sales log on a sturdy clipboard makes a convenient and portable combination.

DAILY SALES LOG

DATE _____   BY _____

PROSPECT	CONTACT PERSON	COMMENTS RESULTS	C A L L	B A C K

CUSTOMER SALES CALL HISTORY

The previous form, the daily sales log, is a chronological calendar and lists daily activities in the order they happen. A customer sales call history is much more specific, as it concentrates on a single prospect or company. It provides a running commentary on each contact and lets you take an overview of all the accumulated sales contacts.

You should note the date and time of the call, the type of call—new customer, regular customer, or follow-up—and the potential for future business—excellent, fair, or poor. You should also write down the name of the person you contacted and note lots of comments. They could prove invaluable to someone else making a follow-up sales call.

CUSTOMER SALES CALL HISTORY

Name _____

Address _____

Phone _____

Key Person _____

Sales Call

Date _____ Time _____
☐ Personal Call   ☐ Telephone
Potential: ☐ Exc ☐ Fair ☐ Poor
Who ?_____
Comments: _____
_____
_____
_____

Follow Date _____

Sales Call

Date _____ Time _____
☐ Personal Call   ☐ Telephone
Potential: ☐ Exc ☐ Fair ☐ Poor
Who ?_____
Comments: _____
_____
_____
_____

Follow Date _____

Sales Call

Date _____ Time _____
☐ Personal Call   ☐ Telephone
Potential: ☐ Exc ☐ Fair ☐ Poor
Who ?_____
Comments: _____
_____
_____
_____

Follow Date _____

Sales Call

Date _____ Time _____
☐ Personal Call   ☐ Telephone
Potential: ☐ Exc ☐ Fair ☐ Poor
Who ?_____
Comments: _____
_____
_____
_____

Follow Date _____

Sales Call

Date _____ Time _____
☐ Personal Call   ☐ Telephone
Potential: ☐ Exc ☐ Fair ☐ Poor
Who ?_____
Comments: _____
_____
_____
_____

Follow Date _____

Sales Call

Date _____ Time _____
☐ Personal Call   ☐ Telephone
Potential: ☐ Exc ☐ Fair ☐ Poor
Who ?_____
Comments: _____
_____
_____
_____

Follow Date _____

Sales Call

Date _____ Time _____
☐ Personal Call   ☐ Telephone
Potential: ☐ Exc ☐ Fair ☐ Poor
Who ?_____
Comments: _____
_____
_____
_____

Follow Date _____

Sales Call

Date _____ Time _____
☐ Personal Call   ☐ Telephone
Potential: ☐ Exc ☐ Fair ☐ Poor
Who ?_____
Comments: _____
_____
_____
_____

Follow Date _____

SECTION III
Doing Business

After you've jumped all of the governmental hurdles, carefully selected the scope and nature of your endeavor, and sized up the competition, it's time to do what you do best. It doesn't matter whether you repair lawnmower engines in you garage, sell merchandise on the party plan, or manage rental units, your business will survive only if you can deal with the day-to-day paperwork required by customers, vendors and governmental agencies.

The following receipts, invoices, cash reports and purchase orders can make your records more accurate and profitable.

JOB ESTIMATES

Most small businesses must sell themselves twice—first as being reputable and capable of doing a job or delivering the service, and once again by doing it at the lowest practical cost. This job estimate form will help you look like the professional you are.

Hint

If your estimate is accepted by a customer, be sure they sign an acceptance.

JOB ESTIMATE

JE- _____

SALES # _____

CUSTOMER # _____

TAX ID # _____

ESTIMATED FOR

_____

_____

_____

WORK LOCATION

_____

_____

_____

YOUR NO.	ORDER DATE	EST. START	EST. FINISH	TERMS

SERVICES	PRICE

TOTAL MATERIAL $	LABOR $	TOTAL EST. $	

THANK YOU FOR THIS OPPORTUNITY

THIS ESTIMATE IS GOOD UNTIL _____

DATE _____ APPROVED BY _____

ACCEPTED BY _____ DATE _____

JOB ESTIMATE

JE- _____

SALES # _____

CUSTOMER # _____

TAX ID # _____

ESTIMATED FOR

_____

_____

_____

WORK LOCATION

_____

_____

_____

YOUR NO.	ORDER DATE	EST. START	EST. FINISH	TERMS

#	MATERIAL	QUANTITY	PRICE EACH	TOTAL PRICE
1				
2				
3				
4				
5				
6				

#	LABOR	RATE	HOURS	AMOUNT
1				
2				
3				
4				
5				

TOTAL MATERIAL $	LABOR $	TOTAL EST. $

THANK YOU FOR THIS OPPORTUNITY

THIS ESTIMATE IS GOOD UNTIL _____

DATE _____ APPROVED BY _____

ACCEPTED BY_____ DATE_____

SALES ORDERS

Once you have a sale, confirm it in writing. A sales order is a multipurpose document that can help in many aspects of a transaction. You can use it to adjust inventory, stimulate your own purchase order for needed material, confirm the terms and conditions of the sale to the customer, or schedule delivery.

SALES ORDER

SALES ORDER # _____

SALES TAX EXEMPTION # _____

TAX IDENTIFICATION # _____

CONFIRMING PHONE # _____

SOLD TO

_____

_____

_____

ATTN: _____

TERMS OF SALE

☐ UPS   ☐ Parcel Post   ☐ Air
☐ Common carrier   ☐ Will call
☐ Other _____
☐ Cash   ☐ Prepaid   ☐ Collect
☐ Promised shipping date   _____
☐ Comments _____
_____

ITEM	QUANTITY	DESCRIPTION	UNIT PRICE	AMOUNT
			TOTAL	

DATE _____   TAKEN BY _____

SALES ORDER

SALES ORDER # _____

SALES TAX EXEMPTION # _____

TAX IDENTIFICATION # _____

CONFIRMING PHONE # _____

SOLD TO

_____

_____

_____

ATTN: _____

TERMS OF SALE

☐ UPS   ☐ Parcel Post   ☐ Air
☐ Common carrier   ☐ Will call
☐ Other _____
☐ Cash   ☐ Prepaid   ☐ Collect
☐ Promised shipping date _____
☐ Comments _____
_____

ITEM	QUANTITY	DESCRIPTION	UNIT PRICE	AMOUNT
			TOTAL	

DATE _____   TAKEN BY _____

SALES ORDER

SALES ORDER # _____

SALES TAX EXEMPTION # _____

TAX IDENTIFICATION # _____

CONFIRMING PHONE # _____

SOLD TO

_____

_____

_____

ATTN: _____

TERMS OF SALE

☐ UPS   ☐ Parcel Post   ☐ Air
☐ Common carrier   ☐ Will call
☐ Other _____
☐ Cash   ☐ Prepaid   ☐ Collect
☐ Promised shipping date _____
☐ Comments _____
_____

ITEM	QUANTITY	DESCRIPTION	UNIT PRICE	AMOUNT
			TOTAL	

DATE _____   TAKEN BY _____

SALES ORDER

SALES ORDER # _____

SALES TAX EXEMPTION # _____

TAX IDENTIFICATION # _____

CONFIRMING PHONE # _____

SOLD TO

_____

_____

_____

ATTN: _____

TERMS OF SALE

☐ UPS   ☐ Parcel Post   ☐ Air
☐ Common carrier   ☐ Will call
☐ Other _____
☐ Cash   ☐ Prepaid   ☐ Collect
☐ Promised shipping date _____
☐ Comments _____
_____

	TOTAL	

DATE _____   TAKEN BY _____

SALES ORDER

SALES ORDER # _____

SALES TAX EXEMPTION # _____

TAX IDENTIFICATION # _____

CONFIRMING PHONE # _____

SOLD TO

_____

_____

_____

ATTN: _____

TERMS OF SALE

☐ UPS   ☐ Parcel Post   ☐ Air
☐ Common carrier   ☐ Will call
☐ Other _____
☐ Cash   ☐ Prepaid   ☐ Collect
☐ Promised shipping date _____
☐ Comments _____
_____

DATE _____   TAKEN BY _____ | TOTAL |

SALES ORDER

SALES ORDER # _____

SALES TAX EXEMPTION # _____

TAX IDENTIFICATION # _____

CONFIRMING PHONE # _____

SOLD TO

_____

_____

_____

ATTN: _____

TERMS OF SALE

☐ UPS   ☐ Parcel Post   ☐ Air
☐ Common carrier   ☐ Will call
☐ Other _____
☐ Cash   ☐ Prepaid   ☐ Collect
☐ Promised shipping date _____
☐ Comments _____
_____

DATE _____   TAKEN BY _____ | TOTAL |

JOB TIME

A big job is often divided into a number of individual tasks. To keep track of job costs, you will need to know how much time and material it takes for each. A job time card follows the work, not the worker. You can examine several job time cards and determine the "value added" of each process step, eventually comparing them to the bid or final sales price of the item or service.

Job time cards are printed three per page and are especially valuable placed on a clipboard and used at the job site.

Hint

These job time cards should not be used as payroll records.

JOB TIME

EMPLOYEE _____

JOB # _____

JOB DESCRIPTION _____

DATE _____

SIGNATURE _____

START TIME	END TIME	START TIME	END TIME	TOTAL TIME	
				HOURS	MINUTES
MATERIAL USED					
COMMENTS					

JOB TIME

EMPLOYEE _____

JOB # _____

JOB DESCRIPTION _____

DATE _____

SIGNATURE _____

START TIME	END TIME	START TIME	END TIME	TOTAL TIME	
				HOURS	MINUTES
MATERIAL USED					
COMMENTS					

JOB TIME

EMPLOYEE _____

JOB # _____

JOB DESCRIPTION _____

DATE _____

SIGNATURE _____

START TIME	END TIME	START TIME	END TIME	TOTAL TIME	
				HOURS	MINUTES
MATERIAL USED					
COMMENTS					

INVOICES AND STATEMENTS

What is the difference between an invoice and a statement? Not much. It is almost a matter of choice. If you don't send out either a statement or an invoice, the results are clear: You'll never get paid. One of the main reasons that small businesses fail is their inability to collect money owed.

The first step to avoid this fate is to bill promptly and in a professional manner. Next is an automatic follow-up routine. Don't be afraid to ask for your money. Otherwise, you may not get it.

INVOICE

INVOICE # I- _____

SALES # _____

CUSTOMER # _____

CUSTOMER TAX ID # _____

SOLD TO

_____

_____

_____

SHIP TO

_____

_____

_____

ITEM	QUANTITY ORDERED	DESCRIPTION	QUANTITY SHIPPED	UNIT PRICE	AMOUNT
		PLEASE PAY ON THIS INVOICE - NO STATEMENT WILL BE SENT			
				SALES TAX	
				TOTAL DUE	

THANK YOU FOR YOUR BUSINESS

DATE _____   APPROVED BY _____

INVOICE

SALES # _____

CUSTOMER # _____

CUSTOMER TAX ID # _____

SOLD TO

_____

_____

_____

SHIP TO

_____

_____

_____

MATERIAL AND LABOR	AMOUNT

PLEASE PAY ON THIS INVOICE - NO STATEMENT WILL BE SENT

SALES TAX	
TOTAL DUE	

THANK YOU FOR YOUR BUSINESS

DATE _____   APPROVED BY _____

75

INVOICE

INVOICE # I- _____

SALES # _____

CUSTOMER # _____

CUSTOMER TAX ID # _____

SOLD TO

_____

_____

_____

SHIP TO

_____

_____

_____

ITEM	QTY./ORDERED	DESCRIPTION	QTY./ORDRD	UNIT PRICE	AMOUNT
		PLEASE PAY ON THIS INVOICE - NO STATEMENT WILL BE SENT			

THANK YOU FOR YOUR BUSINESS

DATE _____   APPROVED BY _____

SALES TAX	
TOTAL DUE	

INVOICE

INVOICE # I- _____

SALES # _____

CUSTOMER # _____

CUSTOMER TAX ID # _____

SOLD TO

_____

_____

_____

SHIP TO

_____

_____

_____

ITEM	QTY./ORDERED	DESCRIPTION	QTY./ORDRD	UNIT PRICE	AMOUNT
		PLEASE PAY ON THIS INVOICE - NO STATEMENT WILL BE SENT			

THANK YOU FOR YOUR BUSINESS

DATE _____   APPROVED BY _____

SALES TAX	
TOTAL DUE	

INVOICE

INVOICE # I- _____

SALES # _____

CUSTOMER # _____

CUSTOMER TAX ID # _____

SOLD TO   SHIP TO

_____   _____

_____   _____

_____   _____

MATERIAL AND LABOR	AMOUNT
PLEASE PAY ON THIS INVOICE - NO STATEMENT WILL BE SENT	

THANK YOU FOR YOUR BUSINESS

DATE _____ APPROVED BY _____

SALES TAX	
TOTAL DUE	

INVOICE

INVOICE # I- _____

SALES # _____

CUSTOMER # _____

CUSTOMER TAX ID # _____

SOLD TO   SHIP TO

_____   _____

_____   _____

_____   _____

MATERIAL AND LABOR	AMOUNT
PLEASE PAY ON THIS INVOICE - NO STATEMENT WILL BE SENT	

THANK YOU FOR YOUR BUSINESS

DATE _____ APPROVED BY _____

SALES TAX	
TOTAL DUE	

STATEMENT

STATEMENT
NUMBER _____

CUSTOMER
NUMBER _____

TO: _____

_____

_____

$ _____

PLEASE DETACH & RETURN THIS PORTION WITH YOUR CHECK

DATE	DESCRIPTION/INVOICE #	CHARGE	CREDIT	BROUGHT FORWARD
			SALES TAX	
			TOTAL DUE	

THANK YOU FOR YOUR BUSINESS

DATE _____   APPROVED BY _____

78

STATEMENT

STATEMENT
NUMBER _____

CUSTOMER
NUMBER _____

TO : _____

_____

_____

$ _____

	BROUGHT FORWARD

	SALES TAX	
	TOTAL DUE	

THANK YOU FOR YOUR BUSINESS

DATE _____ APPROVED BY _____

79

STATEMENT

STATEMENT
NUMBER _____

CUSTOMER
NUMBER _____

TO: _____ $ _____

_____

_____

PLEASE DETACH & RETURN THIS PORTION WITH YOUR CHECK

				BROUGHT FORWARD
DATE	DESCRIPTION/INVOICE #	CHARGE	CREDIT	

THANK YOU FOR YOUR BUSINESS

SALES TAX	
TOTAL DUE	

DATE _____ APPROVED BY _____

STATEMENT

STATEMENT
NUMBER _____

CUSTOMER
NUMBER _____

TO: _____ $ _____

_____

_____

PLEASE DETACH & RETURN THIS PORTION WITH YOUR CHECK

				BROUGHT FORWARD
DATE	DESCRIPTION/INVOICE #	CHARGE	CREDIT	

THANK YOU FOR YOUR BUSINESS

SALES TAX	
TOTAL DUE	

DATE _____ APPROVED BY _____

STATEMENT

STATEMENT
NUMBER _____

CUSTOMER
NUMBER _____

TO: _____ $ _____

_____

_____

PLEASE DETACH & RETURN THIS PORTION WITH YOUR CHECK

	BROUGHT FORWARD
SALES TAX	
TOTAL DUE	

THANK YOU FOR YOUR BUSINESS

DATE _____   APPROVED BY _____

STATEMENT

STATEMENT
NUMBER _____

CUSTOMER
NUMBER _____

TO: _____ $ _____

_____

_____

PLEASE DETACH & RETURN THIS PORTION WITH YOUR CHECK

	BROUGHT FORWARD
SALES TAX	
TOTAL DUE	

THANK YOU FOR YOUR BUSINESS

DATE _____   APPROVED BY _____

RECEIPTS

There is an old saying, "Good fences make for good neighbors." It can be equally applied to money transactions between strangers or even neighbors. Our new saying could be "Good receipts keep good friends together."

We have provided four receipt formats you can use to cover the most common situations. Even if a receipt is just a few lines scribbled on the back of an envelope, it should contain the following items of information.

1) The name of the payor, the person paying out the money.

2) Sufficient identification of the payor, usually the address.

3) The amount of the payment.

4) The date of the transaction.

5) Acknowledgment of payee, the signature of the person receiving the money.

6) Additionally a receipt should contain any other clarifying information that helps identify special conditions such as general conditions of the payment.

    a) "to be credited to account No. "

7) Specific conditions of the payment.

    a) "Rent from January 1, 1988 to January 31, 1988."

    b) "Key deposit and cleaning deposit."

8) General remarks.

    a) "Downpayment on 3 cords of split maple firewood. Balance due Sept 23, 1988."

    b) "Payment in full for lawnmower. Guaranteed for 30 days."

Completion Key

  ① The name of the payor (the person paying the money).

  ② The address (or other identification) of the payor.

  ③ The amount of the payment written in words ("Three Hundred Dollars").

  ④ And again in numerals ($300.00).

  ⑤ The date that the payment is made.

  ⑥ The signature of the person receiving the money.

RECEIPT - General Form   No.

Received From ___①___ , Of ___②___

___ , The Sum Of ___③___ Dollars ___④___ ,

Remarks ___   Dated ___⑤___ , 19 ___

                                      ⑥

RECEIPT - General Form   No.

Received From _ROBERT G. SAMPSON_ , Of _2398 WILLOW AVE._

CONCORD , The Sum Of _THREE HUNDRED_ Dollars _300.00_ ,

Remarks _LAWN KING RIDING_   Dated _MARCH 29_ , 19 88

LAWN MOWER - SOLD "AS-IS"   _Jackson Seller_

RECEIPT - General Form   No.

Received From _____ , Of _____

_____ , The Sum Of _____ Dollars _____ ,

Remarks _____   Dated _____ , 19 __

_____   _____

_____

RECEIPT - General Form   No.

Received From _____ , Of _____

_____ , The Sum Of _____ Dollars _____ ,

Remarks _____   Dated _____ , 19 __

_____   _____

_____

RECEIPT - General Form   No.

Received From _____ , Of _____

_____ , The Sum Of _____ Dollars _____ ,

Remarks _____   Dated _____ , 19 __

_____   _____

_____

RECEIPT - Payment On Account   No.

Received From _____ , Of _____

_____ , The Sum Of _____ Dollars _____ ,

to be Credited to Account No._____   Dated _____ , 19 __

Remarks _____   _____

_____

RECEIPT - Payment On Account   No.

Received From _____ , Of _____

_____ , The Sum Of _____ Dollars _____ ,

to be Credited to Account No._____   Dated _____ , 19 __

Remarks _____   _____

_____

RECEIPT - Payment On Account   No.

Received From _____ , Of _____

_____ , The Sum Of _____ Dollars _____ ,

to be Credited to Account No._____   Dated _____ , 19 __

Remarks _____   _____

_____

RECEIPT - Principal and Interest   No. ____

Received From _____ , Of _____

_____ , The Sum Of _____ Dollars _____ ,

For Payment on Account of which $ _____ is Interest Due to Date, $ _____

is Principal Applied Leaving a New Balance of

$ _____ .   Dated _____ , 19 ___

_____

Remarks _____

RECEIPT - Principal and Interest   No. ____

Received From _____ , Of _____

_____ , The Sum Of _____ Dollars _____ ,

For Payment on Account of which $ _____ is Interest Due to Date, $ _____

is Principal Applied Leaving a New Balance of

$ _____ .   Dated _____ , 19 ___

_____

Remarks _____

RECEIPT - Principal and Interest   No. ____

Received From _____ , Of _____

_____ , The Sum Of _____ Dollars _____ ,

For Payment on Account of which $ _____ is Interest Due to Date, $ _____

is Principal Applied Leaving a New Balance of

$ _____ .   Dated _____ , 19 ___

_____

Remarks _____

RECEIPT - Payment In Full   No.

Received From _____ , Of _____

_____ , The Sum Of _____ Dollars _____ ,

in Payment in Full.   Dated _____ , 19 ___

Remarks _____   _____

_____

RECEIPT - Payment In Full   No.

Received From _____ , Of _____

_____ , The Sum Of _____ Dollars _____ ,

in Payment in Full.   Dated _____ , 19 ___

Remarks _____   _____

_____

RECEIPT - Payment In Full   No.

Received From _____ , Of _____

_____ , The Sum Of _____ Dollars _____ ,

in Payment in Full.   Dated _____ , 19 ___

Remarks _____   _____

_____

STOCK RECORD

If your business maintains an inventory of goods or materials, then it makes good business sense to keep good inventory records. There's nothing magic about it, just a matter of so many in and so many out. The value of inventory control almost vanishes, however, if you are not careful to document each transaction.

STOCK RECORD

ITEM _____ MAIN VENDOR _____ # _____

LOCATION _____ REORDER LEVEL _____ MAXIMUM _____

DATE	COMMENTS	QUANTITY RECEIVED	QUANTITY RELEASED	CARRY FWD
				ON HAND

PURCHASE ORDERS

With cash in hand and a professional-looking purchase order, you can buy almost anything at wholesale cost. This includes saving thousands of dollars on a new car. When you use the business card technique (please refer to the remarks in the first chapter concerning personalization of forms), most firms will readily sell for cash at a wholesale price.

PURCHASE ORDER

PURCHASE ORDER # _____

SALES TAX EXEMPTION # _____

TAX IDENTIFICATION # _____

CONFIRMING PHONE # _____

VENDOR

_____

_____

_____

ATTN: _____

TERMS OF SALE

☐ UPS   ☐ Parcel Post   ☐ Air
☐ Common carrier   ☐ Will call
☐ Other _____
☐ Cash   ☐ Prepaid   ☐ Collect
☐ Comments _____
_____
_____

ITEM	QUANTITY	DESCRIPTION	UNIT PRICE	AMOUNT
				TOTAL

DATE _____   APPROVED BY _____

PURCHASE ORDER

PURCHASE ORDER # _____

SALES TAX EXEMPTION # _____

TAX IDENTIFICATION # _____

CONFIRMING PHONE # _____

VENDOR

_____

_____

_____

ATTN: _____

TERMS OF SALE

☐ UPS   ☐ Parcel Post   ☐ Air

☐ Common carrier   ☐ Will call

☐ Other _____

☐ Cash   ☐ Prepaid   ☐ Collect

☐ Comments _____

_____

_____

ITEM	QUANTITY	DESCRIPTION	UNIT PRICE	AMOUNT
			TOTAL	

DATE _____ APPROVED BY _____

PURCHASE ORDER

PURCHASE ORDER # _____

SALES TAX EXEMPTION # _____

TAX IDENTIFICATION # _____

CONFIRMING PHONE # _____

VENDOR

_____

_____

_____

ATTN: _____

TERMS OF SALE

☐ UPS   ☐ Parcel Post   ☐ Air

☐ Common carrier   ☐ Will call

☐ Other _____

☐ Cash   ☐ Prepaid   ☐ Collect

☐ Comments _____

_____

_____

ITEM	QUANTITY	DESCRIPTION	UNIT PRICE	AMOUNT
			TOTAL	

DATE _____ APPROVED BY _____

PURCHASE ORDER

PURCHASE ORDER # _____

SALES TAX EXEMPTION # _____

TAX IDENTIFICATION # _____

CONFIRMING PHONE # _____

VENDOR

_____

_____

_____

ATTN: _____

TERMS OF SALE

☐ UPS   ☐ Parcel Post   ☐ Air

☐ Common carrier   ☐ Will call

☐ Other _____

☐ Cash   ☐ Prepaid   ☐ Collect

☐ Comments _____

_____

_____

| | TOTAL | |

DATE _____   APPROVED BY _____

PURCHASE ORDER

PURCHASE ORDER # _____

SALES TAX EXEMPTION # _____

TAX IDENTIFICATION # _____

CONFIRMING PHONE # _____

VENDOR

_____

_____

_____

ATTN: _____

TERMS OF SALE

☐ UPS   ☐ Parcel Post   ☐ Air
☐ Common carrier   ☐ Will call
☐ Other _____
☐ Cash   ☐ Prepaid   ☐ Collect
☐ Comments _____
_____
_____

DATE _____ APPROVED BY _____ | TOTAL |

PURCHASE ORDER

PURCHASE ORDER # _____

SALES TAX EXEMPTION # _____

TAX IDENTIFICATION # _____

CONFIRMING PHONE # _____

VENDOR

_____

_____

_____

ATTN: _____

TERMS OF SALE

☐ UPS   ☐ Parcel Post   ☐ Air
☐ Common carrier   ☐ Will call
☐ Other _____
☐ Cash   ☐ Prepaid   ☐ Collect
☐ Comments _____
_____
_____

DATE _____ APPROVED BY _____ | TOTAL |

DAILY CASH REPORT

If there is a common denominator to all businesses, it is the use of cash. Cash is the method of keeping score, and both General Motors Corporation and Bide-a-wee Daycare Center use it as the counting beads of business. Along with keeping score, an accurate daily cash record will help you:

1) Uncover transaction errors in time to correct them and maintain customer goodwill.
2) Double check the amounts being sent to the bank for deposit.
3) Provide figures to post in your general ledger accounts.

Good cash records are an absolute requirement when you try to document business activities for the IRS. The IRS will want to trace every transaction from the customer to the cash record to the entry in the general ledger.

Hint

Depending on your cash volume, you can use this form weekly or even monthly. When you have completed and balanced it, place it and all of the supporting documents into a stout manila envelope for permanent storage. Remember, IRS requires that many business records be retained at least three years, and it wouldn't hurt to add a year or two to be on the safe side.

DAILY CASH REPORT

DATE _____

CASH PAID OUT TO	

LIST CHECK PAY OUTS ON REVERSE

CASH RECEIVED	

CASH COUNT

($___.___CENTS)   ($___.___NICKELS)   ($___.___DIMES)

($___.___QUARTERS) ($___.___HALVES)   ($___.___DOLLARS)

($_____ONES)   ($_____FIVES)   ($_____TENS)

($_____TWENTIES) ($_____FIFTIES) ($_____HUNDREDS)

TOTAL ENDING CASH $

RECAP	
BEGINNING CASH BALANCE	
PLUS CASH RECEIVED	
LESS CASH PAID OUT	
ENDING CASH BALANCE (SHOULD AGREE WITH CASH COUNT ABOVE) OVER OR SHORT	

CHECKS RECEIVED	
TOTAL CHECKS DEPOSITED	
CASH DEPOSITED	
TOTAL DEPOSIT	

PETTY CASH RECORD

Just like a household, a small business may make several small cash purchases each day. Individually, each may not amount to much, but by the end of a week they become very important. The idea behind petty cash is to put a small amount of currency, say $25 or $50, into a cash box. Let's say you need two new batteries for your portable drill. Take the money from petty cash to buy them, fill out the Petty Cash Record, and leave a receipt showing where the money was spent.

When the cash drawer gets low, all of the small transactions are posted to the general ledger at one time. You can post them as one "miscellaneous" entry or as several entries split up into your ledger categories. Recharge the fund with some more currency and you have saved yourself hours in needless bookkeeping drudgery.

Hint

Just because the amounts are small does not mean that your accountant or the IRS does not want to see documentation. Always obtain a receipt, even if it is a grocery store tape with the words "Batteries for drill" written on it and the amount of money circled.

PETTY CASH RECORD

DATE	PAID TO OR RECEIVED FROM	PURPOSE	AMOUNT	CARRY FWD
				BALANCE

RECONCILED BY _____ DATE _____   POSTED BY _____ DATE _____

SECTION IV
Legal Forms

Millions of hours and millions of dollars are spent trying to make transactions bulletproof from legal attack. Even more millions of hours and dollars are later spent trying to iron out differences of opinion. The forms in this section are very general in nature and will fit in straightforward circumstances. If your transaction is complicated, involves a substantial sum of money, or you just don't feel comfortable with a generic form, by all means consult with an attorney.

Before getting into any type of transaction where money is involved, consider the elements of a "contract." They are:

1) An offer.
2) An acceptance.
3) Something of value changing hands. ("Valid consideration" is the legal term.)
4) The parties must have legal "capacity" to enter into a contract.
5) The subject of the contract must be legal.
6) In some cases, the contract must be in writing.

There are miles and miles of "if's, and's, and but's" in the above six statements, but a little common sense helps explain them.

Valid Offer

A valid offer and acceptance are required in any legal contract. Consider a promissory note. A person offers to lend a specific amount of money at a given rate of interest to be repaid under specified terms. The borrower accepts the terms when signing the note and taking up the proceeds of the loan.

Consideration

Consideration or something of value is often a difficult concept to establish, particularly if you stray away from a normal transaction. In a promissory note, for example, the person repaying the loan might have received cash, a tangible item such as a car, or an intangible asset such as the "right" to walk across a neighbor's land.

Legal Capacity

The term deals with issues such as mentally incompetent persons or minor children. Generally speaking, if a person understands the full nature of the transaction, he is usually considered as being responsible for its terms.

Subject

The subject of a contract must in itself be legal. A note signed for a gambling debt between two people cannot be enforced in court since the act of gambling itself is illegal. There are other possible problems in contracts that violate zoning ordinances, permit requirements, consumer protection laws, etc.

In Writing

Finally, and this may surprise you a little, not all contracts need be in writing. Many verbal contracts are perfectly legal, but it would be extremely foolish to rely on this fine point of law. Don't rely on a handshake. Always put it in writing, and always read before you sign.

General Advice

Here are a few points to remember when filling out legal papers.

● Do all of the negotiating *before* you put your name on the dotted line, not after.

● Know whom you are dealing with. If the other party is signing for a company or partnership, is he authorized to bind it? Are signatures of both a husband and wife required?

No contract can be any better than the character and authenticity of the signers. If a legal dispute should result, you'll need to know whether you're dealing with an individual, a partnership, or a corporation.

● Are the terms of the contract legal? Do they comply with consumer and usury (interest rate ceiling) laws in your state?

● Be clear. Spell out the full names of the persons involved and do not use obscure abbreviations.

● After signing, make sure all parties receive fully signed copies of the paper and check out any special witness requirements. Where appropriate, we recommend the best signature format.

Signature and Witnessing Formats

This book contains several forms that are legal in nature that *must* be witnessed in some cases, and *should* be witnessed in others. We will talk about this when each legal form is presented.

Any discussion of signature and witnessing requirements could be quite complicated and beyond the scope of this book. For example: A properly filled out and signed (but not witnessed or notarized) Power of Attorney form should be completely legal and acceptable anywhere in the country.

The exception to this is when the power deals with real estate, and then it must be notarized. If, however, a merchant, banker, or legal adviser is not personally acquainted with the persons involved, it might be difficult to verify the authenticity of the signature. This could mean that a perfectly legal document might be useless.

Simple Signature(s)

The easiest of all signature formats is a straightforward signature(s) with a date and no witness lines.

Signature with Witness(es)

The second format consists of signature(s) and one or two witnesses. The witness confirms the identity and mental capacity of the signer. No person who is a party to the transaction—for example, the buyer in a Bill of Sale—should be a witness.

Acknowledgment by Notary Public

The final and perhaps the most complicated format is a formal acknowledgment by a notary public. A notary public is a person, usually "appointed" by the governor of your state, who acknowledges, attests, or certifies documents under an official seal. A notary also takes affidavits and depositions.

The services of a notary public is required in some documents (affidavits and anything to do with real estate), is recommended in some (powers of attorney), and is quite unnecessary in others (most promissory notes). The notary usually sees the signature being applied to the paper.

When requesting acknowledgment from a notary who does not know you personally, be prepared to produce adequate identification, such as a driver's license. A notary public can be found in most financial, real estate, or insurance offices. They may charge a dollar or two for their service.

Completion Key

A number of forms use terms that may not be familiar to you. To insure that you understand how to fill out each form, particularly legal ones, this book provides both a filled-out sample and a translation into plain English of any term or blank that might be confusing. This book uses what we call "completion keys" to do that. They are signified by a number inside a circle, as in the examples on the opposite page.

Good Advice

These are important legal forms. Fill in all of the appropriate blanks *before* you sign.

AFFIDAVIT

An affidavit is a voluntary written statement of facts made before a person legally authorized to administer an oath or affirmation. Generally, affidavits are sworn before a notary public but can be made before judges, clerks of the court, commissioners, or justices of the peace.

Most states require that a valid affidavit consist of four parts:

1) A statement of the place where the affidavit is taken.

2) A statement of the facts.

3) The signature of the person (the affiant) making the statement.

4) Evidence that the affidavit was properly made before an authorized person—normally a notary public.

There are a number of instances where an affidavit can be sworn. For example, "On February 25, 1984, I lost my wallet containing my driver's license and other identification. I discovered it missing on the evening of the same day and think it was lost in the neighborhood of 2nd and Main streets. The loss has been reported to the police."

Completion Key

① Your full name.

② The statement of facts to which you are swearing.

③ Your normal signature.

④ Reserved for specific language by Notary Public.

Remember, acknowledgment by a notary public is required when completing this form.

Hint

This is a serious document. You could be charged with perjury if you make a false statement in an affidavit.

AFFIDAVIT

State of _____

County of _____

_____①_____ , of the City of _____ ,

County of _____ , State of _____ , being

duly sworn on his oath, disposes and says:

That:

②

③

④ State of _____ , County of _____

Subscribed and sworn to before me this _____ day of _____ , 19 ____

by _____ .

(Seal)

_____
(Signature of notarial officer)

My commission expires ___/___/___   NOTARY PUBLIC

AFFIDAVIT

State of _NEW HAMPSHIRE_

County of _MERRIMACK_

AMANDA G. WILSON , of the City of _CONCORD_ ,

County of _MERRIMACK_ , State of _NEW HAMPSHIRE_ , being

duly sworn on his oath, disposes and says:

That: ON FEBRUARY 25, 1988, I LOST MY WALLET CONTAINING LICENSE AND OTHER IDENTIFICATION. I DISCOVERED IT MISSING ON THE EVENING OF THE SAME DAY AND THINK IT WAS LOST IN THE NEIGHBORHOOD OF 2ND AND MAIN STREETS. THE LOSS HAS BEEN REPORTED TO THE POLICE.

Amanda H. Wilson

State of _NEW HAMPSHIRE_ County of _MERRIMACK_

Subscribed and sworn to before me this _22ND_ day of _MARCH_ , 19 _88_

by _AMANDA G. WILSON_

(Seal)

Jo Ann Gilbert
(Signature of notarial officer)

My commission expires _MAR/25/89_   NOTARY PUBLIC

AFFIDAVIT

State of _____

County of _____

_____ , of the City of _____ ,

County of _____ , State of _____ , being

duly sworn on his oath, disposes and says:

That:

_____

State of _____ , County of _____

Subscribed and sworn to before me this _____ day of _____ , 19 _____

by _____ .

(Seal)

_____
(Signature of notarial officer)

My commission expires _____ / _____ / _____   NOTARY PUBLIC

AGREEMENT

A simple handshake can be good enough between good friends or trusted business colleagues, but a handshake is often not a good basis on which to settle a disagreement in court. An agreement usually starts with "I'll do this if you do that." When in doubt, put it in writing.

An agreement does not have to be witnessed or signed before a notary public, except if the document deals with real estate. Most documents relating to real estate transactions should be notarized and recorded.

Completion Key

① The date of this agreement.

② It takes two to agree, or disagree. Some legal forms call them the party of the first part and the party of the second part. Put the name of the first person(s) here.

③ For proper indentification, enter a full address, including the county or parish of residence of the first party.

④ The name of the second person(s) involved in the agreement.

⑤ The address, including county or parish, of the second party.

⑥ What the first party agrees to do.

⑦ What the second party agrees to do.

⑧ The signature of the first party.

⑨ The signature of the second party.

AGREEMENT

THIS AGREEMENT, made ___①___, 19___, is between ___②___

_____ of ___③___

and_____③_____ ___④___ of ___⑤___

_____, who agree as follows:

⑥ ⑦

The effective date of this agreement is _____, 19___

_____ ⑧

_____ ⑨

AGREEMENT

THIS AGREEMENT, made JULY 23, 19 88, is between JOHNATHAN S. WILLIAMSON of 2364 SAND PIPER DRIVE, OCEAN PARK, WA and SAM SILBERMAN of 9933 BAY ROAD OYSERVILLE, WA, who agree as follows:

JOHNATHAN S. WILLIAMSON AUTHORIZES SAM SILBERMAN TO CUT DOWN SIX DOUGLAS FIR TREES LOCATED ON WILLIAMSON'S PROPERTY ON SAND PIPER DRIVE.

SAM SILBERMAN AGREES TO CUT DOWN THE MARKED DOUGLAS FIR TREES, CUT THEM INTO 16" LENGTHS, AND SPLIT THEM INTO FIREWOOD. SILBERMAN WILL DELIVER ONE HALF OF THE WOOD TO WILLIAMSON'S GARAGE, KEEPING THE OTHER HALF FOR HIMSELF.

SILBERMAN AGREES NOT TO DAMAGE ANY OTHER TREES ON THE PROPERTY.

SILBERMAN AGREES THAT THIS WORK WILL BE DONE BY NOT LATER THAN SEPT 1ST, 1988.

The effective date of this agreement is JULY 23, 19 88

Johnathan S. Williamson

Sam Silberman

AGREEMENT

THIS AGREEMENT, made _____ , 19 _____ , is between _____

_____ of _____

and _____ of _____

_____ , who agree as follows:

The effective date of this agreement is _____ , 19 _____

_____

_____

BILL OF SALE

A bill of sale is an agreement in writing in which a person sells the rights and title to, and interest in, an item of personal property to another. This form *should not* be used in real estate transactions. If you are buying or selling an automobile, use the special bill of sale in the automobile section of this book.

A bill of sale:

1) Identifies the buyer and seller.

2) Puts the agreed price in writing.

3) Describes the property.

4) States that the seller is the owner and that the goods are free and clear from any mortgages, liens, security interests, or encumbrances.

You should demand a bill of sale when involved in any transaction of either substantial value or questionable ownership. For instance, a bill of sale would not be appropriate when buying garage sale bric-a-brac, but might be valuable when purchasing an expensive, used 10-speed bicycle from a stranger.

Two versions of a bill of sale are provided. The first is for use by an individual, and the second where the property is jointly owned by two people.

Completion Key

① The name of the seller—the first seller where the property is jointly owned.

② The address of the seller.

③ The name of the buyer.

④ The address of the buyer.

⑤ The sales price.

⑥ A complete and accurate description of the item(s) sold.

⑦ Any mortgages, liens, encumbrances, or security interests. If none, write "None."

⑧ Date of sale.

⑨ Signature of seller.

BILL OF SALE

Individual Seller

I ____①____, seller, of ____②____,

City of _____, County of _____, State of

_____, acknowledge receipt from ____③____,

buyer, of ____④____, City of _____, County of

_____, State of _____, the sum of $ ____⑤____,

representing full payment, and hereby sell and deliver to the buyer the following described property:

⑥

Seller is the lawful owner of the goods and the goods are free from all liens or security interests except:

⑦

Dated ____⑧____, 19____ ____⑨____

BILL OF SALE

Individual Seller

I ROSE A. WILLIAMSON, seller, of 414 VISTA,

City of AKRON, County of LAKE, State of

OHIO, acknowledge receipt from BOB E. SMITH,

buyer, of 39 MAPLE, City of AKRON, County of

LAKE, State of OHIO, the sum of $1,250.00,

representing full payment, and hereby sell and deliver to the buyer the following described property:

ONE WURLITZER 3-KEY BOARD ORGAN

MODEL 1245

SERIAL # 145682-1

Seller is the lawful owner of the goods and the goods are free from all liens or security interests except:

NONE

Dated DEC 18, 19 88 Rose Williamson

BILL OF SALE

Individual Seller

I, _____, seller, of _____,

City of _____, County of _____, State of _____,

_____, acknowledge receipt from _____,

buyer, of _____, City of _____, County of

_____, State of _____, the sum of $_____

representing full payment, and hereby sell and deliver to the buyer

the following described property:

Seller is the lawful owner of the goods and the goods are
free from all liens or security interests except:

Dated _____, 19 _____

_____

BILL OF SALE

Community property or joint ownership

We, _____, and

_____, of _____,

City of _____, County of _____, State of

_____, acknowledge receipt from _____,

buyer, of _____, City of _____, County of,

_____, State of _____, the sum of $_____

representing full payment, and hereby sell and deliver to the buyer

the following described property:

Sellers are the lawful owners of the goods and the goods
are free from all liens or security interests except:

Dated _____, 19 _____

_____

PROMISSORY NOTES

A promissory note is a contract in which one person promises to pay at agreed terms and conditions. (It's really a lot more complicated but this will have to do for our purposes). There are three major versions of a promissory note in this book—demand, installment, and installment with balloon payment.

A *balloon* is a larger payment at the end of a note. For example, a balloon note could call for 35 payments of $100 and the balance ($5,000) due as the 36th payment. This is quite common in real estate financing. Each of these categories is in turn broken down into wording for individual borrowers and joint (community) borrowers.

The terms *lender* and *borrower* are used in the text. A lender can also be a seller in a transaction where an item of property changes hands rather than an advance of loan proceeds. Conversely, the term borrower would include the buyer in the same type of transaction.

On Demand

A promissory note that is on demand contains the following important points.

1) The parties are individual persons, not corporations.

2) The note is due and payable at the demand of the lender.

3) The interest of the note will be due and payable on a specified schedule—monthly, quarterly, annually, etc.

4) Should the lender have to sue the borrower, the borrower will have to pay all reasonable legal fees.

Installment Note

An installment note contains the following important points:

1) The parties are individual persons, not corporations.

2) The principal or interest may not be demanded by the lender except as to the exact terms in the note.

3) Principal and interest payments will be due and payable on a specified schedule—monthly, quarterly, etc.

4) If the borrower fails to make a payment, the remaining principal and interest owing can be declared due and payable.

5) Should the lender have to sue the borrower, the borrower will have to pay all reasonable legal fees.

Completion Key

① The amount of the note written in numerals ($575.00).
② The place (City & State) where the note is drawn.
③ The date that the note is drawn.
④ The name(s) of the lenders or sellers.
⑤ The address of the lenders or sellers.
⑥ The amount of the note written out in words (Five Hundred Seventy-Five).
⑦ The interest rate of a note written out in words (Twelve percent).
⑧ The interest rate written in numerals (12%).
⑨ The schedule of interest payments—monthly, quarterly, semi-annually, or annually.
⑩ The signature(s) of the borrower(s). Normally, witnessing or acknowledgment by a notary public is not necessary on promissory notes.

Hint

These documents can be used for making loans to corporations. Use the individual format, and the borrower should print the company name, the word "by," followed by the signature and title of the corporate officer.

PROMISSORY NOTE - ON DEMAND

$ ___①___

② _____
③ _____ , 19 ___

On demand, for value received, I promise to pay to the order of ___④___ ,
at ___⑤___ , City of _____ ,
County of _____ , State of _____ ,
the sum of ___⑥___ Dollars ($ ___①___), with interest
thereon at the rate of ___⑦___ percent (___⑧___ %) per annum, payable
___⑨___ thereafter.

In the event of a lawsuit to enforce payment of this note, I agree to pay such additional sum as attorney's fees as the court may adjudge reasonable, both at trial and on appeal.

___⑩___

PROMISSORY NOTE - ON DEMAND

$ 575.00

CONCORD
MAR 23 , 19 88

On demand, for value received, I promise to pay to the order of DONALD G. WILLISON ,
at 7321 MAPLE LANE , City of CONCORD ,
County of MERRIMACK , State of NEW HAMPSHIRE ,
the sum of FIVE HUNDRED SEVENTY-FIVE Dollars ($ 575.00), with interest
thereon at the rate of TWELVE percent (12 %) per annum, payable
MONTHLY thereafter.

In the event of a lawsuit to enforce payment of this note, I agree to pay such additional sum as attorney's fees as the court may adjudge reasonable, both at trial and on appeal.

Henry J. Jola

PROMISSORY NOTE - ON DEMAND

$ _____

_____

_____ , 19 _____

On demand, for value received, I promise to pay to the order of _____ ,

at _____ , City of _____ ,

County of _____ , State of _____ ,

the sum of _____ Dollars ($ _____), with interest

thereon at the rate of _____ percent (_____ %) per annum, payable

_____ thereafter.

   In the event of a lawsuit to enforce payment of this note, I agree to pay such additional sum as attorney's fees as the court may adjudge reasonable, both at trial and on appeal.

_____

PROMISSORY NOTE - ON DEMAND

$ _____

_____

_____ , 19 _____

On demand, for value received,

we jointly and severally promise to pay to the order of _____ ,

at _____ , City of _____ ,

County of _____ , State of _____ ,

the sum of _____ Dollars ($ _____), with interest

thereon at the rate of _____ percent (_____ %) per annum, payable

_____ thereafter.

    In the event of a lawsuit to enforce payment of this note, we agree to pay such additional sum as attorney's fees as the court may adjudge reasonable, both at trial and on appeal.

_____

_____

PROMISSORY NOTE - INSTALLMENT

$ _____

_____

_____ , 19 _____

For value received, I promise to pay to the order of _____ ,

at _____ , City of _____ ,

County of _____ , State of _____ ,

the sum of _____ Dollars ($ _____), with interest

thereon at the rate of _____ percent (_____ %) per annum, payable in

_____ equal monthly installments of _____ , Dollars

($_____) beginning on _____ , 19 _____ .

In the event of default of any of the installments as herein provided, time being of the essence, the holder of this note may without notice or demand declare the entire principal sum then unpaid, together with accrued interest thereon immediately due and payable.

In the event of a lawsuit to enforce payment of this note, I agree to pay such additional sum as attorney's fees as the court may adjudge reasonable, both at trial and on appeal.

_____

PROMISSORY NOTE - INSTALLMENT

$ _____

_____

_____ , 19 _____

For value received,

we jointly and severally promise to pay to the order of _____ ,

at _____ , City of _____ ,

County of _____ , State of _____ ,

the sum of _____ Dollars ($ _____), with interest

thereon at the rate of _____ percent (_____ %) per annum, payable in

_____ equal monthly installments of _____ , Dollars

($_____) beginning on _____ , 19 _____ .

In the event of default of any of the installments as herein provided, time being of the essence, the holder of this note may without notice or demand declare the entire principal sum then unpaid, together with accrued interest thereon immediately due and payable.

In the event of a lawsuit to enforce payment of this note, we agree to pay such additional sum as attorney's fees as the court may adjudge reasonable, both at trial and on appeal.

_____

_____

112

POWER OF ATTORNEY

A power of attorney is a powerful legal instrument and is often a key part of estate planning. It authorizes someone else, either an individual or a financial institution, to act as your agent and sign your name for you. You are called the *principal* and the person or institution whom you have authorized to sign for you is called your *agent* or *attorney-in-fact*.

In some states, your attorney-in-fact has the power—and an implied duty—to act on behalf of you in the event of incapacity. If you were to suffer a heart attack, or be involved in a serious accident, there may be hours, days, or even weeks when you do not have the physical or mental capacity to handle your own personal and legal affairs. In some states, your attorney-in-fact's power to act for you during your incapacity must be stated in the power of attorney. Our form provides for that.

In other circumstances, some occupations and situations keep a person from being available to handle important day-to-day matters. For example, in some states, the spouse of a person away in military service would not be able to sign a simple installment contract for a new hot water heater without having a valid power of attorney.

A person granting a power of attorney has a number of flexible choices. He or she can:

1) Grant a general power of attorney, one that allows the agent to act in almost all circumstances on behalf of the principal.

2) Grant a special or limited power of attorney. This allows the agent to act only in limited affairs as set out in the document.

3) Appoint an alternate in case the agent dies or is incapacitated. This is important and is often part of the estate-planning process.

4) Control delivery of the power of attorney by placing it with an attorney or other representative to be delivered only upon certain events—serious illness, unusual or dire circumstances, etc.

5) Alter, change, or cancel the power at any time. The death of the principal automatically cancels a power of attorney.

The mere fact that your power of attorney was signed many years ago does not invalidate it, but it does frequently raise questions from those who may be dealing with your agent. It is a good idea to renew them occasionally.

A power of attorney should be witnessed or notarized. It also should be recorded at the county courthouse in the following situations:

● If it is to be used by your agent to transfer an interest in real estate. It should be recorded in the county where the real property is located.

● Occasionally, a bank, stock transfer agent, title insurance company, or other institution will insist on having the original or a certified copy. You or your agent should always keep the original. If a photocopy is not acceptable, then record the power of attorney with the county recording department and purchase a certified copy. Once your power of attorney is recorded, you or your agent can always order additional certified copies, no matter how much time has elapsed since it was recorded.

● If you or your agent are concerned about losing the original power of attorney, then record it. Once it is recorded, there will be less need for the original.

General Power of Attorney

A general power of attorney is exactly as the name implies. It grants to another person the full general power to perform each and every act that you could legally do. The person granted this power can even pass it on to another. Should you desire to have the power of attorney be in effect only in the event of your physical incapacity, then we suggest that you put it in the hands of the family attorney or other trusted personal representative.

Limited Power of Attorney

A limited power of attorney authorizes one to act for another only in some limited circumstances. Be sure to list the limitations carefully and clearly. An example of a limitation would be "To bid and purchase stock on my behalf at the Mt. Ivy Cattle Auction." In this example, you would probably want to enter a specific ending date for the power.

Completion Key

① The name of the person giving the power of attorney, the principal.
② The principal's address.
③ The name of the person receiving the power, the agent or attorney-in-fact.
④ The agent's address.
⑤ The limitations.
⑥ A specific date. If you want the power of attorney to run until revoked in writing, then draw a line through the space. This indicates that you deliberately choose not to have a specified date.
⑦ The signature of the principal, the person giving the power of attorney. It is recommended that all powers of attorney be acknowledged before a notary public.

LIMITED POWER OF ATTORNEY

I, _____①_____ of _____②_____, City of _____, County of _____, State of _____ hereby constitute and appoint _____③_____ of _____④_____, City of _____, County of _____, State of _____, my true and lawful attorney in fact for me and in my name, place, and stead, giving unto my attorney in fact full power to do and perform all and every act that I may legally do through and attorney in fact, for the following limited purpose(s) and for no other

_____
_____⑤_____
_____

I hereby grant my attorney in fact every power necessary to carry out the limited purposes for which this power of attorney is granted.

This power of attorney shall not be affected by and shall continue in full force and effect during my subsequent disability or incompetency.

The rights, powers, and authority of my attorney in fact herein granted shall commence and be in full force and effect from the date I sign this power of attorney and such rights, powers, and authority shall remain in full force and effect thereafter until ____⑥____, 19____, or revoked by me in writing.

Dated _____, 19____   _____⑦_____

- -
(OPTIONAL)

State of _____, County of _____

This instrument was acknowledged before me on _____,

by _____.

_____
(Signature of notarial officer)

My commission expires ___/___/___   NOTARY PUBLIC

LIMITED POWER OF ATTORNEY

I, DONALD L. WILLISON of 7321 MAPLE VIEW, City of AKRON, County of LAKE, State of OHIO hereby constitute and appoint BRENDA L. WILLISON, of 7321 MAPLE VIEW, City of AKRON, County of LAKE, State of OHIO, my true and lawful attorney in fact for me and in my name, place, and stead, giving unto my attorney in fact full power to do and perform all and every act that I may legally do through and attorney in fact, for the following limited purpose(s) and for no other

TO PURCHASE PROPERTY AT AUCTIONS
IN 1988

I hereby grant my attorney in fact every power necessary to carry out the limited purposes for which this power of attorney is granted.

This power of attorney shall not be affected by and shall continue in full force and effect during my subsequent disability or incompetency.

The rights, powers, and authority of my attorney in fact herein granted shall commence and be in full force and effect from the date I sign this power of attorney and such rights, powers, and authority shall remain in full force and effect thereafter until JANUARY 1, 19 89, or revoked by me in writing.

Dated JULY 9, 19 88   Donald L Willison

- -
(OPTIONAL)

State of _____, County of _____

This instrument was acknowledged before me on _____,

by _____.

_____
(Signature of notarial officer)

My commission expires ___/___/___   NOTARY PUBLIC

GENERAL POWER OF ATTORNEY

I, _____ of _____ , City of
_____ , County of _____ , State of _____ .
hereby constitute and appoint _____ ,
of _____ , City of _____ , County of
_____ , State of _____ , my true and lawful
attorney in fact for me and in my name, place, and stead, giving unto my attorney in fact full power
to do and perform all and every act that I may legally do through an attorney in fact, and every
proper power necessary to carry out the purposes for which this power is granted, with full power
of substitution and revocation, hereby ratifying and affirming that which attorney in fact or any
substitute shall lawfully do or cause to be done by virtue of this power of attorney and the powers
it grants.

This power of attorney shall not be affected by and shall continue in full force and effect during
my subsequent disability or incompetency.

The rights, powers, and authority of my attorney in fact herein granted shall commence and
be in full force and effect from the date I sign this power of attorney and such rights, powers,
and authority shall remain in full force and effect thereafter until _____ , 19 _____ , or
revoked by me in writing.

Dated _____ , 19 _____   _____

- -

(OPTIONAL)

State of _____ , County of _____

This instrument was acknowledged before me on _____ ,

by _____ .

_____
(Signature of notarial officer)

My commission expires _____ / ____ / _____   NOTARY PUBLIC

LIMITED POWER OF ATTORNEY

I, _____ of _____ , City of

_____ , County of _____ , State of _____

hereby constitute and appoint _____ ,

of _____ , City of _____ , County of

_____ , State of _____ , my true and lawful
attorney in fact for me and in my name, place, and stead, giving unto my attorney in fact full power
to do and perform all and every act that I may legally do through and attorney in fact, for the
following limited purpose(s) and for no other

_____

_____

_____

I hereby grant my attorney in fact every power necessary to carry out the limited purposes
for which this power of attorney is granted.

This power of attorney shall not be affected by and shall continue in full force and effect during
my subsequent disability or incompetency.

The rights, powers, and authority of my attorney in fact herein granted shall commence and
be in full force and effect from the date I sign this power of attorney and such rights, powers,
and authority shall remain in full force and effect thereafter until _____ , 19 _____, or
revoked by me in writing.

Dated _____ , 19 _____   _____

- -
(OPTIONAL)

State of _____ , County of _____ .

This instrument was acknowledged before me on _____ ,

by _____ .

_____
(Signature of notarial officer)

My commission expires _____ / / _____   NOTARY PUBLIC

REVOCATION OF POWER OF ATTORNEY

When you have drawn a power of attorney, you may, at any time, revoke it. This form simply withdraws any powers granted to an attorney-in-fact. You should make sure that you have proof that this revocation has been received by your agent. If you record the power of attorney in the courthouse, you should also record the revocation.

Completion Key

① The name of the principal, the person who gave the power of attorney and who now wants to revoke it.

② The address of the principal.

③ The date of the original power of attorney.

④ The name of your attorney-in-fact, the person to whom you gave the power.

⑤ The address of the attorney-in-fact.

⑥ If you are revoking a general power of attorney, check the first box, and if you are revoking a limited power, insert about the same wording used on the original.

⑦ The date that the revocation is in effect.

⑧ Your signature. It is recommended that revocations be acknowledged before a notary public.

REVOCATION OF POWER OF ATTORNEY

I, ____①____ of ____②____, City of _____, County of _____, State of _____, did in writing on ____③____, 19____, appoint ____④____ of ____⑤____, City of _____, County of _____, State of _____.

⑥ (check one)

☐ my true and lawful general attorney-in-fact and,
or
☐ my true and lawful attorney-in-fact to _____, and

do hereby annul, cancel, revoke, and terminate all rights, powers, authorities, privileges, and immunities set out in that power of attorney.

Dated ____⑦____, 19____　　____⑧____

(OPTIONAL)

State of _____, County of _____

This instrument was acknowledged before me on _____

by _____

_____
(Signature of notarial officer)

My commission expires ____/__/__　　NOTARY PUBLIC

REVOCATION OF POWER OF ATTORNEY

I, DONALD L. WILLISON of 7321 MAPLE VIEW LANE, City of CONCORD, County of MERRIMACK, State of NEW HAMPSHIRE, did in writing on AUGUST 1, 19 87, appoint BRENDA H. FIGINNI, of 3473 OAK CREST LANE, City of CONCORD, County of MERRIMACK, State of NEW HAMPSHIRE.

(check one)

☒ my true and lawful general attorney-in-fact and,
or
☐ my true and lawful attorney-in-fact to ____
TO PURCHASE FIVE HEAD OF
STOCK AT THE MT. IVY CATTLE
AUCTION, and

do hereby annul, cancel, revoke, and terminate all rights, powers, authorities, privileges, and immunities set out in that power of attorney.

Dated AUG 5TH, 19 87　　Donald L. Willison

(OPTIONAL)

State of NEW HAMPSHIRE, County of MERRIMACK

This instrument was acknowledged before me on AUGUST 5, 1987

by DONALD L. WILLISON

JoAnn Gilbert
(Signature of notarial officer)

My commission expires JUNE / 8 /87　　NOTARY PUBLIC

REVOCATION OF POWER OF ATTORNEY

I, _____ of _____ , City of

_____ , County of _____ , State of _____ , did

in writing on _____ , 19 _____ , appoint _____ ,

of _____ , City of _____ , County of

_____ , State of _____ ,

(check one)

☐   my true and lawful general attorney-in-fact and,
or
☐   my true and lawful attorney-in-fact to _____

_____

_____

_____ , and

do hereby annul, cancel, revoke, and terminate all rights, powers, authorities, privileges, and immunities set out in that power of attorney.

Dated _____ , 19 ____   _____

(OPTIONAL)

State of _____ , County of _____

   This instrument was acknowledged before me on _____ ,

by _____ .

                                        _____
                                        (Signature of notarial officer)

My commission expires _____ / ____ / _____   NOTARY PUBLIC

RENTAL AGREEMENTS

Many business have cars or equipment not used 100% of the time to produce income. You can earn substantial extra income by occasionally negotiating a short-term rental agreement. Potential losses can be minimized by knowing the person you are doing business with. Use the credit application form provided in this book to acquire the information you need to check out the borrower's credit reputation.

Such arrangements can be financially rewarding by earning an extra income to help pay for the considerable maintenance costs of owning a business vehicle or equipment. There are dangers, however. First, check with your insurance agent. You will want to doublecheck that you are completely covered at all times.

Another important consideration is the condition of the property. If you simply "lend" to a friend for a few hours, you are only required to display so-called ordinary care and diligence. If you rent a unit, however, you may be required to exercise "extraordinary" care and diligence. The key is to keep good maintenance records, conduct a careful joint inspection of the equipment, and put everything in writing. These forms will help.

RENTAL AGREEMENT

The date of this agreement is _____ , 19 _____ and is between _____

_____ , of _____ ,
        (Owner)   (Owner's Address)

and _____ of _____ .
            (Renter)   (Renter's Address)

PROPERTY

The property Owner agrees to rent is (describe):

_____

_____

_____

_____

In the following paragraphs, the term "property" will mean the above described property plus any equipment provided or attached to it.

To the best of Owner's knowledge, the property is free from defects that would affect safe and reliable operation under normal and prudent usage.

INSPECTION

Note any defects:

_____

_____

_____

_____

Fluid Levels
Gas/Diesel
Oil
Propane

_____

E	1/4	H	3/4	F

PERIOD OF RENTAL

The Owner agrees to rent this property to the Renter from _____ (AM)(PM) on _____ ,

19 _____ to _____ (AM)(PM) on _____ , 19 _____ .

INDEMNITY

The Renter shall fully indemnify the Owner for all damage to or loss of the property during the term of this agreement, except damage arising from deficiencies in the rented equipment.

THE USE OF THIS PROPERTY

A. The operator(s) shall be limited to _____

_____

and Renter warrants that the above person(s) have the skills and all valid licenses required to safely and legally operate this property.

B. The Renter agrees:

    1. not to use the property for commercial purposes,
    2. not to use the property beyond the rate capacity,
    3. to use the property in accordance to manufacturer's instructions,
    4. not to remove or dismantle any equipment from the property,
    5. not to operate the property in a hazardous manner,
    6. to operate the property in accordance with all local, state, and federal laws,
    7. and not to use the property for any illegal activity.

C. The Renter agrees that the property shall be used only within the following areas:

_____

_____

INSPECTION

The Owner shall have the right to inspect the property at any reasonable time.

RENTAL RATE

The Renter shall pay the Owner at the rate of $ _____ per _____ plus all fuel and oil used during the course of the rental period.

DEPOSIT

The Renter shall pay a deposit of $ _____ which shall be used to pay for loss or damage to the property during the term of this agreement. If there is no loss or damage, the deposit shall be credited as a payment against the rental fee and any excess returned to the Renter.

RETURN

The property shall be returned to the Owner at _____ by no later than _____ . The level of all fluids shall be equal to those indicated at the beginning of the rental period.

TERMINATION

The Owner shall have the right to terminate this agreement at any time if the Renter violates any of its terms. Upon termination the Renter shall promptly return the property to the Owner.

_____
(Renter)

_____
(Renter)

_____
(Owner)

SECTION V
Landlording Forms

Many thousands of people own one or more rental units. And most of them could save time and money by keeping better records. Some enter the landlording business because they inherited a unit with tenants, and some bought rentals as investments. Still others were forced into it by not being able to sell their house when moving to another city. Studies have shown that millions of dollars are lost by owners making three common mistakes:

1) Renting to the WRONG tenant.
2) Keeping the WRONG tenant after you've rented to him or her.
3) Doing the WRONG things after the tenant has left.

In this section we supply more than 20 helpful (and sometimes vital) forms that should help prevent some of these errors. Many of these forms are accompanied by text and some hints. Please take a moment to read these comments as they make using the form or worksheet easier and more meaningful.

We have not included the most important document in the whole process—a basic landlord/tenant agreement. Many states have unique landlord/tenant laws, and it's not prudent to supply you with a one-size-fits-all agreement.

If your rental situation is complex, we strongly urge that you consult with an attorney for an agreement that best protects your interests. If you feel comfortable with a "standard" agreement or one that has been "localized" for your jurisdiction, then look for one in a local stationery store or print shop. Some larger metropolitan areas and most states have trade associations for landlords and property managers. These groups could be an excellent resource for locally acceptable leases and rental agreements.

Using These Forms

Like many other of the business forms in this book, most of the following are designed to be personalized with a business card. For best results, review the information in the first chapter of this book.

APPLICATION FOR RENTAL

The first step in the rental process is qualifying the prospective renter. Think of the landlord/tenant relationship as a credit transaction. After all, a landlord places an asset worth tens of thousands of dollars into the hands of a stranger, in short, a loan of the value of the dwelling unit. No one needs to remind you of the cost of selecting a non-paying, malicious, or destructive tenant.

Most landlords have simple requirements. They usually want a tenant who can and will make regular rental payments and who will take reasonable care of the property. There is no magic wand to wave that helps in the selection decision. There is, however, some advice that has been around in the credit business for decades. Any loan applicant (prospective tenant) must be of good character and have the capacity to meet the terms of the Rental Agreement.

"Character" in this context simply means the desire to honor monthly commitments. It is very difficult to judge a person's future actions without some reference to his or her past. This is why it is important to get a completely filled-out rental (credit) application.

Having the capacity to pay rent simply means that the tenant has a steady source of income sufficient to meet all family obligations, including the rent. Capacity can be verified by checking the applicant's employment record and making a judgment as to the potential of continued employment in his or her business or occupation.

Here are several important points to consider when reviewing a prospective tenant's application:

Name

Be sure to get the renter's full name. It is difficult to locate Jim Smith when you are really dealing with Robert James Smith.

Date of Birth

If you plan to secure a credit report, the reporting agency will require adequate identification. The renter's date of birth, social security number, driver's license number, etc., all contribute to this positive identification.

Addresses

Note that both the present and the previous address are required. They help in the identification process and establish the stability of the prospect.

Landlord Information

This could be the most important section of the whole application. After all, the treatment of previous landlords is an excellent indicator. The answers should be straightforward, and easy to verify. Be on guard for fraudulent names—relatives, close friends, etc.—and be prepared to spend a few dollars in long-distance calls.

Employment Information

Data concerning employment will give you some indication of the tenant's stability and ability to make and continue monthly payments on time. If the applicant has hedged on this or other bits of information, be alert. There may be hidden facts.

Credit References

These are primarily for use by a credit bureau, but you can check them directly if you wish.

Emergency Numbers

These names (usually relatives) are important for "skip tracing" should the renter disappear.

Roommate/Spouse

A little extra information cannot hurt, particularly when you're trying to find a tenant. You can also gain extra protection by having spouses and roommates sign all the documents of the Rental Agreement.

Discrimination Laws

As a landlord, you may not refuse to rent to people because of their race, creed, color, national origin, sex, or marital status. This does not mean that you have to rent to anyone that comes along with first and last months' rent money in hand. It is perfectly permissible to set your own reasonable rental standards. Once set, however, your standards must be applied equally to all applicants and not selectively because of the race, creed, color, etc. of the prospective renter. You should have no problem if your policy is in writing and you apply it fairly and equally to all.

Setting Standards

Here are a few things to consider when setting minimum rental standards:

● Income-to-rent ratio may not be more than 25% (or some other reasonable number) of the family's gross income.

● The credit report must be of reasonable scope and contain no derogatory information.

● There must be at least sic months (or one year) of steady, current employment.

● Satisfactory references from previous landlords must be verified going back two full years.

● Maximum number of tenants in the unit.

● Lifestyle guidelines, such as non-smokers only, no pets, no waterbeds, number of vehicles on the premises and so on.

Remember that you may apply any guidelines that you deem reasonable, but you must apply them consistently.

Hint

If you need help in securing a credit report on your prospective tenant, look in the Yellow Pages under "Credit Reporting Bureaus" or "Credit Bureaus." They usually list a consumer information number.

Remember that by signing this document, the tenant authorizes you to investigate his or her credit background. And you promise to keep any information you get confidential. Be sure that you do.

APPLICATION FOR RENTAL

PLEASE PRINT --- ALL information must be completed. The decision to rent to you will depend in great part on your credit history and references. Use the back for additional information.

PERSONAL INFORMATION

Full Name _____ Home Phone _____ Work Phone _____

DOB _____/_____/_____ Soc. Sec. _____—_____—_____ Driver's License _____ State _____

Present Address _____ City _____ State _____ Zip _____

How Long? _____ If rent, apartment name _____ Phone _____

    Landlord/mgr's name _____ Alternate Phone _____

    Why are you leaving? _____

Previous Address _____ City _____ State _____ Zip _____

    How Long? _____ Apartment name _____ Phone _____

    Landlord/mgr's name _____ Alternate Phone _____

Employer _____ Position _____ How Long? _____

    Address _____ Gross income before deductions _____

Former Employer _____ How Long? _____

    Address _____ Phone _____

CREDIT REFERENCES

Bank _____ Acct #(s) _____ Branch _____

    City _____ State _____ How long _____ Check _____ Save _____ Loan _____

Other active reference _____ Acct # _____

    City _____ State _____ How long _____ Check _____ Save _____ Loan _____

EMERGENCY-In an emergency you may contact - (List two other than spouse)

Name _____ Relationship _____ Phone _____

    Address _____ City _____ State _____

Name _____ Relationship _____ Phone _____

    Address _____ City _____ State _____

    List all motor vehicles, including recreational vehicles, to be kept at the dwelling unit on the reverse. Include make, model, year, and license plate number.

Page 1 of 2 - Please continue on next page.

SPOUSE-ROOMMATE PERSONAL INFORMATION

Full Name _____ Home Phone _____ Work Phone _____

DOB ____ / ____ / ____ Soc. Sec. _____ — ____ — _____ Driver's License _____ State _____

Present Address _____ City _____ State _____ Zip _____

How Long? _____ If rent, apartment name _____ Phone _____

　　　　Landlord/mgr's name _____ Alternate Phone _____

Employer _____ Position _____ How Long? _____

　　　Address _____ Gross income before deductions _____

CREDIT REFERENCES

Bank _____ Acct #(s) _____ Branch _____

　　City _____ State _____ How long _____ Check _____ Save _____ Loan _____

Other active reference _____ Acct # _____

　　City _____ State _____ How long _____ Check _____ Save _____ Loan _____

EMERGENCY–In an emergency you may contact - (List one other than spouse)

Name _____ Relationship_____ Phone_____

　　Address _____ City _____ State _____

OTHER INFORMATION

OTHER PERSONS (INCLUDING CHILDREN) WHO WILL LIVE IN THE DWELLING UNIT

Name _____ age _____ Name _____ age _____
Name _____ age _____ Name _____ age _____

Type and breed of pets to be kept at dwelling unit. _____
Do you have a waterbed? ☐ Yes ☐ No   If yes, waterbed insurance? _____
Have you ever been evicted? _____ If yes, explain

I (we) declare that the above statements are correct and I (we) give my (our) permission for any credit reporting agency to release my credit file to undersigned Landlord solely for the purposes of entering into a Rental Agreement. I (we) further authorize the Landlord or his Authorized Agents to verify the above information including but not limited to contacting creditors, both listed herein or not, present or former landlords, and personal references.

Applicant: _____

Dated _____ , 19 _____

Applicant: _____

I certify that any verifications are for the purpose of entering into a Rental Agreement and I further agree that any information derived from credit reports and other verifications will be kept confidential and not revealed to any outside party.

Dated _____ , 19 _____　　Landlord: _____

PET AGREEMENTS

Next to nonpayment, nothing causes more anguish for owners than the damage and disturbance created by dogs and cats. There are many documented cases where damage has run into thousands of dollars for new carpet, repainting, and replacement of doors and woodwork—and this doesn't even take into account inside residual odors or the exterior damage to yard and garden.

While a landlord can never be 100% sure of being able to enforce pet rules and regulations, there is a much better chance of an effective landlord/resident relationship if everything is spelled out in writing.

These agreements should be considered as additions to the basic landlord/tenant agreement. Make sure tenants understand that you consider these agreements to be very important and you will take action if they are ignored.

Hint

Spayed and neutered pets have a much lower potential for damage than those without these operations. You can recognize this reality and encourage your tenants by having a lower pet deposit for spayed females and neutered males.

PET AGREEMENT
(SPAYED OR NEUTERED)

This agreement is part of a Rental Agreement dated _____ , 19____ between Landlord(s) _____ and _____ .

and

the Resident(s) _____ and _____ .

That the Resident has paid and the Landlord acknowledges receipt of a special pet security/cleaning deposit of $ _____ .

That the Landlord gives permission for the Resident to maintain pet(s), of the following types or breeds _____ in the above dwelling unit.

Any female pet MUST BE SPAYED (incapable of producing a litter). Any male pet MUST BE NEUTERED.

The Resident agrees that both the pet security/cleaning deposit and the regular security/cleaning deposit may be used to cover special costs associated with pets. These include, but are not limited to:

a.   Carpet cleaning.
b.   Carpet replacement.
c.   Room and carpet deodorizing
d.   Damaged drapes.
e.   Scratched doors, walls, and furniture.
f.   Flea and pest control.

The Resident agrees not to keep "exotic" or other pets generally known as wild. The Resident further agrees not to keep any dog generally known as vicious or difficult to control.

The Resident agrees to keep and maintain the pet(s) in a manner that will not disturb the peace and quiet of other Residents and neighbors. Excessive barking by dogs will not be allowed and the Resident will be expected to keep the yard, sidewalks, and common areas clear of animal waste.

Violation of this agreement will entitle the Landlord to terminate the Rental agreement.

Dated _____ , 19 _____ Resident _____

Resident _____

Dated _____ , 19 _____ Landlord _____

PET AGREEMENT

This agreement is part of a Rental Agreement dated _____ , 19 _____ between Landlord(s)

_____ and _____ .

and

the Resident(s) _____ and _____ .

That the Resident has paid and the Landlord acknowledges receipt of a special pet security/cleaning deposit of $ _____ .

That the Landlord gives permission for the Resident to maintain pet(s), of the following types or breeds _____
in the above dwelling unit.

Should a pet produce a litter, the Resident may keep them at the dwelling unit for no more than six weeks past weaning.

The Resident agrees not to engage in any commercial activities concerning the buying or selling of animals.

The Resident agrees that both the pet security/cleaning deposit and the regular security/cleaning deposit may be used to cover special costs associated with pets. These include, but are not limited to:

a. Carpet cleaning.
b. Carpet replacement.
c. Room and carpet deodorizing.

d. Damaged drapes.
e. Scratched doors, walls, and furniture.
f. Flea and pest control.

The Resident agrees not to keep "exotic" or other pets generally known as wild. The Resident further agrees not to keep any dog generally known as vicious or difficult to control.

The Resident agrees to keep and maintain the pet(s) in a manner that will not disturb the peace and quiet of other Residents and neighbors. Excessive barking by dogs will not be allowed and the Resident will be expected to keep the yard, sidewalks, and common areas clear of animal waste.

Violation of this agreement will entitle the Landlord to terminate the Rental agreement.

Dated _____ , 19 _____ Resident _____

Resident _____

Dated _____ , 19 _____ Landlord _____

If, as the old saying goes "Good fences make for good neighbors," then allocated parking places make for even better and friendlier neighbors. You can easily put parking restrictions in writing by using these two parking agreements. Two different agreements are provided, one for a single car and one for two cars. They list the exact place where parking is allowed, discuss guest parking, and list any fees.

Always be sure to exchange signed copies of this and any other agreement.

Hint

When going over parking agreements with tenants, it is best to discuss recreational vehicles. You would be surprised at the "forgetfulness" of a tenant who has parked a dilapidated old camper in the driveway of your unit.

PARKING AGREEMENT
(Single vehicle)

This agreement is part of a Rental Agreement dated _____ , 19 _____ between Landlord _____ , of _____ , _____ , _____ .

and

the Resident(s) _____ , and _____ ,
of _____ , _____ , _____ .

The Resident agrees to pay to the Landlord a fee of $_____ each month for the following specific parking privileges and further agrees to the following:

That a _____ , (description of auto) or its replacement may park at any time at _____
(description of parking place).

That any vehicle parked at this location must be operable. Disabled cars will be towed.

That guests may temporarily park _____ ,

That boats and other recreational vehicles may;

☐ NOT be stored or kept on premises.   ☐ be parked or stored at the following location:

_____

The Resident agrees to the following additional conditions:

_____
_____
_____
_____

Violation of this agreement will entitle the Landlord to terminate the Rental agreement.

Dated _____ , 19 _____ Resident _____

Resident _____

Dated _____ , 19 _____ Landlord _____

PARKING AGREEMENT
(Two vehicles)

This agreement is part of a Rental Agreement dated _____ , 19 _____ between Landlord
_____ , of _____ , _____ ,
_____ .   and

the Resident(s) _____ , and _____ ,
of _____ , _____ , _____ .

The Resident agrees to pay to the Landlord a fee of $_____ each month for the following specific parking privileges and further agrees to the following:

That _____ , (description of auto) or its replacement may park at any time at _____ (description of parking place) and that _____ , (description of auto) or its replacement may park at any time at _____ (description of parking place).

That any vehicle parked at this location must be operable. Disabled cars will be towed.

That guests may temporarily park _____ ,

That boats and other recreational vehicles may;

☐ NOT be stored or kept on premises.   ☐ be parked or stored at the following location:

_____

The Resident agrees to the following additional conditions:

_____
_____
_____
_____

Violation of this agreement will entitle the Landlord to terminate the Rental agreement.

Dated _____ , 19 _____ Resident _____

Resident _____

Dated _____ , 19 _____ Landlord _____

WATERBED AGREEMENT

Waterbeds, if improperly installed or abused, can cause thousands of dollars in damages. You can reduce losses due to waterbeds by insisting on certain minimum requirements. You can also insure against most potential losses by insisting that your tenants obtain waterbed insurance coverage. These policies are readily available through most insurance agents or even some waterbed stores.

Hint

To avoid future misunderstandings, make sure your basic rental agreement clearly states that waterbeds are not permissible unless agreed to in writing.

WATERBED
AGREEMENT

This agreement is part of a Rental Agreement dated _____ , 19 _____ between Landlord
_____ , of _____ , _____ ,
_____ .

and

the Resident(s) _____ , and _____ ,
of _____ , _____ , _____ .

Residents are authorized to maintain a waterbed under the following limitations and restrictions:

1. The waterbed will be of material at least 20 mils in thickness and be encased in a saftey liner of at least 8 mils in thickness.

2. The waterbed will be located only in a place approved by the Landlord.

3. The waterbed will be installed per manufacturers' specifications.

4. The Residents agree to allow the Landlord to inspect the waterbed at any reasonable time.

5. The Residents agree to purchase a waterbed insurance policy with a policy limit of at least $100,000 naming Landlord as beneficiary.

6. The Residents agree to pay immediately for any damage caused by their waterbed.

The Resident has paid and the Landlord acknowledges receipt of a special waterbed security/damage deposit of $_____ .

Violation of this agreement will entitle the Landlord to terminate the Rental agreement.

Dated _____ , 19 _____ Resident _____

Resident _____

Dated _____ , 19 _____ Landlord _____

INVENTORY OF FURNISHINGS

An inventory of furnishings is necessary only when you rent a unit partially or fully furnished. If the unit is equipped only with a few appliances, you can use the Move-in/Move-out Inspection Report that follows. Completeness and clarity can help eliminate future misunderstandings.

Carefully maintain the original while giving a signed copy to the renter. When going through the move-out process, tick each item in the right-hand column of the form and fully describe any damage on the back. Where damage to the unit or furnishings is unusually severe, photographs or, better yet, video tapes provide excellent backup documentation. This type of additional evidence can be very worthwhile in the event of a lawsuit.

INVENTORY OF FURNISHINGS

Dwelling Unit Address: _____

Resident: _____ Inventory Date _____ , 19 _____

ROOM	ITEM	NUM	COMMENTS	MOVE OUT

Page _____ of _____

Resident agrees that this represents an accurate inventory and description of the current condition and assumes responsibility for these items in the dwelling unit as of _____ , 19 _____ .

MOVE IN   MOVE OUT

_____ Date _____   _____ Date _____

_____ Date _____   _____ Date _____

MOVE-IN/MOVE-OUT INSPECTION REPORT

A landlord can claim any damage—excluding fair wear and tear—against security/cleaning deposits or later in a lawsuit. The residents, however, may counter that the damage was there prior to their moving in. Except in cases of extreme and gross damage, the pre-existing defense is difficult to fight unless good documentation is provided. This form is a very important part of that documentation.

There can be no substitute for spending a few moments with the resident and going through the unit room by room. In fact, ask the tenant to fill out the report and mark any comments. If the comments cannot fit in the space provided, mark "See reverse" and elaborate on the back.

Hint

This form can double as an inventory of built-in kitchen appliances. Every line should have something written on it, including "NA"—meaning not applicable.

MOVE-IN / MOVE-OUT
INSPECTION REPORT

Dwelling Unit Address: _____

Resident: _____ Inspection _____ , 19 _____

		MOVE-IN	COMMENTS	MOVE-OUT
G E N E R A L	Paint-walls-ceilings			
	Pet odor-damage			
	Smoke detectors			
	Entry bell & light			
	Patios			
	Yard, garden, etc.			
	Windows, drapes, screens			
K I T C H E N	Stove			
	Oven			
	Refrigerator			
	Disposal & dishwasher			
	Cupboards & counters			
	Sinks			
	Carpets - floors			
	Doors & locks			
	Fixtures & lights			
	Switches & outlets			
L R D R	Carpets - floors			
	Doors & locks			
	Fixtures & lights			
	Switches & outlets			
B R M S	Carpets - floors			
	Doors & locks			
	Fixtures & lights			
	Switches & outlets			
B A T H S	Carpets - floors			
	Doors & locks			
	Fixtures & lights			
	Switches & outlets			
	Shower-sink-tub			
	Dripping faucets			
K E Y S	Front door key(s)			
	Back door key(s)			
	Garage key(s)			
	Other key(s)			

Resident agrees that this represents an accurate description of the current condition and assumes responsibility for the dwelling unit as of _____ , 19 _____ .

MOVE-IN

_____ Date _____

MOVE-OUT

_____ Date _____

MEMO TO RENTER

A notice from a landlord (usually bad news) can be up-beat and friendly if put in the right format. This form helps you communicate those small items concerning such things as rule changes or minor maintenance in a non-threatening, but structured way.

This form prints two to a page. By using carbon paper and a clipboard, you can easily keep copies of your memos.

MEMO

TO _____   _____
                                                                DATE

Just a note to let you know that:

_____

_____

_____

_____

_____

_____

Thank you,

MEMO

TO _____   _____
                                                                DATE

Just a note to let you know that:

_____

_____

_____

_____

_____

_____

Thank you,

DWELLING UNIT INSPECTION REQUEST

Most rental agreements include a clause to the effect that "Both the Landlord(s) and Resident(s) agree to allow the Landlord, with 48 hours written notification, to enter the dwelling unit at reasonable hours to inspect, make repairs, or show the unit to prospective residents."

This letter puts the tenants on notice in a pleasant way that you wish to inspect the unit for specific purposes. It suggests that if the time and date are not convenient, you should be contacted to set up a more suitable time.

DWELLING UNIT
INSPECTION REQUEST

TO: _____   _____ , 19 _____

_____

_____

       It would be appreciated if you would allow entry into your dwelling unit
on _____ , 19 _____ at _____ (AM) (PM) for
the purposes of:

☐   Showing the unit to prospective residents.

☐   Inspect the unit for general and preventative maintenance
requirements.

☐   Repair/replace the following:

_____

_____

_____

☐   To _____

_____

_____

       If the above time is not convenient, please contact so we may set another
time and date.

Sincerely,

_____
Landlord

NOTICE OF CHANGE OF TERMS

Rental rates are usually set out in the basic rental agreement, but the agreement usually contains provisions to make changes in the rates. This form notifies the resident of your intention to increase rates and sets the effective date.

The rental agreement will set the notice provision, usually 30 days. To stay within the law, you must abide by these limitations. You can improve renter/landlord relations by giving renters the benefit of a longer notice period than required.

NOTICE OF CHANGE OF TERMS

Date_____

TO _____

_____

_____

☐ CERTIFIED MAIL

\# _____

☐ Hand Delivered

☐ Regular Mail

You are hereby notified that the tems of tenancy under which you occupy the above described property are to be changed as follows:

Effective _____ / _____ / _____ , your rent will increase by $ _____ per month for a total of $_____ each month.

_____

Landlord

ANNUAL LETTER

Owners with the good fortune to have considerate and promptly paying tenants should do everything possible to keep things that way. Sending a gentle, once-a-year reminder of some of the important terms of the rental agreement can be a useful management tool.

This annual letter serves several purposes. First, it reminds them of pet and waterbed restrictions. It jogs their memory that you do not carry insurance on their personal possessions, only the building. Finally, this letter asks your tenants to make a safety check of all the smoke detectors in the unit.

Hint

Date, sign, and keep a copy of each letter sent. This evidence of careful management could be important in the event of a legal dispute.

ANNUAL LETTER

Date _____

TO _____

      _____

      _____

Every year, we like to remind our tenants of several important issues.

1) Please remember that we carry insurance coverage ONLY on the building. Our policies do not cover personal possessions such as your furniture, clothing, etc. Nor do our policies cover any damage caused by your own negligence. If you desire to have personal coverage for these risks, we strongly suggest that you contact your own personal insurance agent.

2) Please conduct a safety check of all smoke detectors located in the unit. If any detector needs new batteries, we will be most willing to provide them.

3) Our Rental Agreement calls for the following limitations on maintaining pets at the premises:

    ☐ Pets are NOT permitted.
       The maintenance of pets at the premises is limited to:

      _____

      _____

If these conditions are not being met, you must comply immediately.

4) Our Rental Agreement calls for the following limitations on installing waterbeds on the premises:

    ☐ Waterbeds are NOT permitted.
       The installation of waterbeds is limited to:

      _____

      _____

If you have a waterbed not specifically covered in writing, please contact us immediately. If you have an authorized waterbed, please remember that we require that you maintain a standard waterbed insurance policy with policy limits not less than $100,000.

5) _____

_____

_____

_____

_____

Thank you,

_____

Landlord

STATEMENT

Many owners send monthly statements of rental due. Although not absolutely necessary, statements do help minimize the "Oh, I forgot it's the first of the month" excuse.

Hint

Statements are printed two to a page. You can save a bit of time by copying a dozen or so in advance and using them as the need arises.

STATEMENT

TO _____   _____
                                                          Transmittal date
_____
_____

Statement

Notice of rent due by _____ _____

For period _____ _____ to _____ _____

Thank you,

STATEMENT

TO _____   _____
                                                          Transmittal date
_____
_____

Statement

Notice of rent due by _____ _____

For period _____ _____ to _____ _____

Thank you,

FIRST AND SECOND NOTICES

One of the strongest weapons in the landlord's collection arsenal is predictability. Delinquency, even if it is just a few days, should be treated as a serious matter. Once the landlord establishes a pattern of immediate reaction to a late payment, "slow-pay" residents may well put rent a little higher on their payment priority list.

Collection experts recommend that a first notice be sent between three and five days after the due date and a second notice between seven and ten days. Where a renter has a history of serious delinquency, the second notice might be dropped in favor of an even stronger, three-day notice to pay or vacate.

Hint

Do not continually threaten eviction unless you intend to follow through. It loses its effectiveness on the tenants and may make later eviction even more difficult.

A REMINDER

Date _____

TO _____
_____
_____

Just a reminder that your rent was due on _____ . Rent more than _____ days past the due date requires a late charge payment of $ _____ and an additional $ _____ per day thereafter.

PLEASE . . . . take care of this matter immediately.

Thank You,

_____
Landlord

VERY IMPORTANT

Date _____

TO _____
  _____
  _____

Your rent is now PAST DUE since _____ . As of this date, the delinquent rent and late charges total $ _____ .

You MUST settle this account or all other legal options will have to be considered.

PLEASE . . . . take care of this matter immediately.

Thank You,

_____
Landlord

A three-day notice clearly indicates that matters are extremely serious and that the landlord is only interested in bringing rent to current status. This form may not conform to the laws in some states where specific landlord/tenant statutes have been enacted. If this is the case, the landlord should secure either the proper format from an attorney or a form sold at a reputable legal stationery store.

Hint

Where the case is very serious, send this notice by Certified Mail. Be sure to keep a copy of this and all other correspondence to prevent a tenant's "No notice" defense.

NOTICE TO PAY RENT OR VACATE

Date _____

TO _____   ☐ CERTIFIED MAIL

_____   # _____

_____   ☐ HAND DELIVERED

YOU ARE HEREBY NOTIFIED THAT THE RENT FOR THE PERIOD _____, 19___ to _____, 19___ is now past due. As of this date, the total sum owing, including late charges is $ _____ . Unless this sum is received by the undersigned within three days of this notice, you will be required to vacate and surrender the premises.

If it becomes necessary to institute legal action for the non-payment of rent or to obtain possession of the dwelling unit, as per the terms of the Rental Agreement, you will be liable for recovery of our reasonable attorney fees and expenses. You will also be liable for any rental fees for the time you are in possession of the dwelling unit.

_____
Landlord

NOTICE TO VACATING RESIDENTS

The best opportunity to settle the numerous moving-out details is as soon as possible after receiving notice. This letter will set a businesslike tone to the settlement process. It should be used in combination with the Move-in/Move-out Recap and Deduction Schedule that follows.

This notice to vacating residents confirms the move-out date, asks that the unit be left in good condition, sets out the funds being held by the landlord, asks that the unit be made available to be shown to prospective tenants, and requests an appointment to inspect the rental unit.

NOTICE TO VACATING RESIDENTS

TO: _____   _____ , 19 _____

_____

_____

Dear Resident:

Thank you for your notice (received _____ ,19 _____) that you intend to move out of the dwelling unit effective _____ , 19 _____ .

It will be necessary for you to vacate the unit by no later than 12:00 midnight of the effective date.

Please insure the dwelling unit is in the same condition as when you moved in - fair wear and tear excepted.

Your Rental Agreement allows the Landlord to show the dwelling unit to prospective Residents at convenient times. Your cooperation would be appreciated.

Since a final inspection must be made, please:

☐ Contact me at your earliest convenience to set an appointment prior to your departure date, or

☐ I/we will visit the dwelling unit at _____ AM/PM on _____ , 19 ____.

_____

_____

_____

_____

_____

Thank you.

_____
Landlord

MOVE-IN/MOVE-OUT RECAP AND DEDUCTION SCHEDULE

This form is designed to be used either separately or with the "Notice to Vacating Residents." It notifies the resident of several important conditions:

1) That notice has been received.

2) That as of a specified date, a certain amount of funds are on hand in the form of deposits and advance rent.

3) That as of a specified date, a certain amount will be due (rent, late charges, etc.).

4) That the landlord expects the dwelling unit to be in similar condition as when rented.

5) That potential charges may be for any damage beyond fair wear and tear.

Hint

You will probably need two of these forms. The first, marked "Initial," should be sent when you receive the first notice and the second, marked "Final," for the final accounting when all costs are computed.

MOVE-IN / MOVE-OUT RECAP
AND DEDUCTION SCHEDULE
☐ Initial ☐ Final

Dwelling Unit Address _____

Resident _____   Move-in date _____ , 19 _____

Notice received _____ , 19 _____   Move-out date _____ , 19 _____

Funds on hand as of _____ .   Disposition as of _____

Key deposit	$ _____.____	Rent due _____ to _____	_____.____
Security/clean deposit	_____.____	Late charges due	_____.____
Pet clean-up deposit	_____.____	NSF charges due	_____.____
Other _____	_____.____	Key charge	_____.____
Other _____	_____.____	Cleaning charge	_____.____
Other _____	_____.____	Repairs/replacements	_____.____
Other _____	_____.____	Other _____	_____.____
TOTAL	$ _____	TOTAL	$ _____.____

Due FROM Resident   ($ _____.____)

or

Refund Due TO Resident $ _____.____

Forwarding Address _____

_____   _____
(Landlord)   Receipt acknowledged (Resident)

Date _____   Date _____

REPRESENTATIVE DEDUCTION SCHEDULE

The following items and charges are averages only and should not be considered as actual minimums or maximums. They point out the cost of excessive damage or the lack of cleanliness. There will be no charge if the dwelling unit is left in the original move-in condition, allowing for fair wear and tear.

Appliance repair - labor	$25 to 100	General clean per room	$10 to 35
Appliance parts	At cost	Key - door	3 to 5
Appliance cleaning	10 to 20	Key - mailbox	3 to 5
Cabinet repair (each)	10 to 50	Locks - replace	10 to 25
Cabinet replace	At cost	Painting per room	15 to 50
Carpet shampoo per room	15 to 35	Pet damage	At cost
Carpet repair	At cost	Rubbish - haul away	10 to 50
Doors	At cost	Sink, tub, toilet - clean	10 to 15
Drapes stained	15 to 25	Sink, tub, toilet - replace	At cost
Drapes replace	At cost	Sheetrock damage	At cost
Fire exting - recharge	10 to 25	Smoke detector	10 to 35
Fire exting - replace	25 to 75	Windows broken	25 to 100

NOTICE OF ABANDONED PROPERTY

Little can be more aggravating than a tenant's leaving property behind (almost always of little or no value). This is often the case in a forced eviction or where there has been an unpleasant relationship between the renter and the tenant. If you carelessly dispose of abandoned property, even though it is totally worthless, you leave yourself open to serious mischief by a tenant seeking revenge.

The whole area of abandoned property is very sensitive and laws vary from state to state. If there is obvious substantial value to the property, and you are not familiar with the regulations of your state, a consultation with a qualified attorney could be in order.

This notice of abandoned property sets out to carefully describe the property, state a date certain for action, and clearly note what will happen to the property. If your tenant has left a junker car, you should contact the local Department of Motor Vehicles for information on the best way to dispose of it. In many areas, junkyards are not allowed to accept a car unless it is accompanied by a valid and signed-off certificate of title, but almost all states have provisions for the routine disposal of abandoned or worthless hulks.

Most jurisdictions require proof that a good-faith effort was made to contact the rightful owner of the property. Always send this notice to the last known address, preferably one provided by the tenant in the rental application or other, more recently signed document.

NOTICE OF ABANDONED PROPERTY

Date _____

TO _____   ☐ CERTIFIED MAIL
   _____   # _____
   _____

When you vacated the rental unit located at _____
you left the following described property at the premises:

_____

_____

_____

_____

_____

Unless claimed and removed by no later than _____ , 19 ____ , the above described
will be:

☐   Thrown away.

☐   Given to a charitable organization (Goodwill, Salvation Army, etc.).

☐   Sold in a manner prescribed by law with the proceeds first used to cover the costs of
    the sale, then to cover any sums due, and with the remainder returned to you.

☐   _____
    _____
    _____
    _____

Thank you for your immediate attention to this matter,

_____
Landlord

RECEIPTS—RENT/INCIDENTALS

In addition to the receipts in Section III of this book, two more specialized receipts are provided especially for landlording. Your records deserve the extra time it takes to create a receipt, and your tenant will probably insist on one completely and properly filled out.

RECEIPT - RENT   No. _____

Received from _____ , of _____

_____ , The Sum of* _____ Dollars $(_____),

in rent for the period _____ , 19 ____ to _____ , 19 ____

for residence located at _____ .

* Includes late charge of $ _____

Remarks _____   Dated _____ , 19 ____

_____   _____

RECEIPT - RENT INCIDENTALS   No. _____

Received from _____ , of _____

_____ , The Sum of _____ Dollars $(_____),

for residence located at _____ .

☐ First Months rent from _____ , 19 ____ to _____ , 19 ____ $ _____
☐ Last _____ Month(s) rent $ _____   ☐ Utilities Deposit $ _____
☐ Key Deposit $ _____   ☐ Pet Deposit $ _____
☐ Waterbed Deposit $ _____   ☐ Security / Cleaning $ _____
☐ _____ $ _____   ☐ _____ $ _____

Remarks _____   Dated _____ , 19 ____

_____   _____